Tales from the Bat Cave

by
Ovid J. McLaughlin

First published by AuthorHouse 03/25/05

ISBN: 1-4208-2200-4 (sc)

Printed in the United States of America
Bloomington, Indiana

This book is printed on acid-free paper.

authorHOUSE™

1663 Liberty Drive, Suite 200
Bloomington, Indiana 47403
(800) 839-8640
www.AuthorHouse.com

~ ACKNOWLEDGMENTS ~

I would like to express my thanks to all of the fellow Officers of the Toledo Police Department, who shared their time and stories with me as I worked on this book.

I also would like to dedicate this book in memory of my parents, Raymond and Mary Jane McLaughlin, who believed in me during my tenure as a Police Officer and as a son.

To my wife Karen, let it be said that without all her love, support and encouragement, I would never have amounted to anything.

My daughters, Julie and Jaime, who have been, and still are, my pillars of strength throughout my career and whom I had to sacrifice so very much of their growing up because of the hours I had to work.

To Father Mike Madden who guided me through the days of humiliation that I suffered at the end of my career and who is my "angel" sent from above.

To Doctor Thomas Oweiss, the surgeon at St. Luke's Hospital. If he had not been there in the Emergency Room on that near fatal day in 2001, I would not have been here to complete this project.

Julius "Jeep" Materni, my first real partner, who was involved in many of these stories and who is one of the few who have remained a close friend, even after we have retired.

Jerry "Bubba" Bryce, a brother Officer and one of my best and closest friends, who left this life too soon on September 12, 1987. I miss him and think about him each and every day.

Bob Jones, the television crime reporter from Channel 11, WTOL, who treated me like a human being, instead of a criminal. He granted my wishes and did not push me for interviews during my tribulations at the end. He is a true professional and compassionate person, as far as I am concerned.

And finally, to Diane at Proof Plus in Connecticut. Without her assistance, guidance, perseverance, and dedication with this project, I would still be setting at my desk with a bunch of notes.

Dedication

To all brother police officers from the Toledo Police Department past, present and future, whom without, these stories could not have been told. To my partners over the years, as we lived these stories together. To the newer officers and the future officers: remember to write down notes, so your stories can be told or remembered through the years. They will be some of the best stories of your life.

Explanation of "Bat Cave"

During the mid-1960's and early 1970's, an expressway was being built in and around the City of Toledo, Ohio. Certain sections of the expressway opened before others were completed. One particular section was in the western part of the city and was about three-quarters of a mile in length. It connected two busy streets in the western part of the city, such as Talmadge Road on the west end and Secor Road at the east end. This section of the expressway was on the western edge of our patrol district. We were receiving several complaints of persons using this section of the expressway for "drag racing" during the late night or early morning hours.

To combat this problem, we felt we needed a place to be able to sit undetected and watch what was going on. We found that if we backed up after entering from Talmadge Road eastbound until we were under the overpass, we could watch vehicles westbound and eastbound and these vehicles would not be able to see us.

7

Many times, we would sit there and finish our reports for the night, etc. When any unlawful activity would occur on this section of the expressway, we were able to take care of it immediately.

After learning of our place of concealment, the dispatchers named it the "Bat Cave". "Batman and Robin" was a very popular television show at the time. Many times, when the dispatcher needed our location, he would ask if we were in or near the "Bat Cave".

There were times that a Command Officer would ask the location of such "Bat Cave" and the dispatcher would inform him, "That said location is on their district and I will let you know where it is, if you will call by phone, but I do not want to put it out over the air, thus putting their location in jeopardy."

So many of these stories came into conversation while my partners and I reminisced, as we sat in the "Bat Cave" awaiting unlawful activity.

Explanation of the Era of these Stories

I would like everyone reading these stories to please remember that most events occurred many years ago. The weapons that were carried by Police Officers were .38 caliber revolvers, before the use of portable radios, air conditioning in the police vehicles, copy machines, and computers. Even the sirens on the vehicles had to be activated by flicking a switch and then pressing on the horn rim. Sirens on the paddy wagons were on the fenders of the vehicles and, during the winter, the sirens would freeze. Many times, we would throw hot water, coffee, or whatever was available, to thaw the sirens out so they would work. The light on top of the police vehicles was one revolving red light and the vehicles were black and white. Police reports were three copies and two sheets of carbon paper were used for each report. Police shirts were gray in color, starched heavily, with brass buttons that had to be attached with metal clips on the back each time you changed shirts. So, as you read these stories, remember the time period.

~ Table of Contents ~

In The Beginning

*A*ll through High School, in the late 1950's, I had played football and wrestled competitively. My dream was to go to college and then come back to my high school and coach the football team. Those dreams went by the wayside during my first year at college.

My dad was a sheet metal worker and, most of the time, worked outside in the elements. The economy that year was horrible, along with a terribly cold and wet winter. Being a sheet metal man, dad was unable to work much that year and my family had not saved money for college education like parents do today. In those days when you had your high school diploma, you were considered well set on finding a good job that you stayed at for the rest of your life.

While in high school, every Friday night, a sock hop was held at the YMCA in the west part of the town and it drew students from all over the city. There were usually eight to ten police officers working off-duty to keep everyone in line. This was before drugs hit the scene. In those days, every once in a while, one of the kids would get intoxicated on 3.2% beer before coming to the dance. When they got out of line, it would be brought to one of the officer's attention and the officer would take some action. Unless the kid really got unruly, the officer would escort him home; if not, they would send him downtown to the juvenile facility. In this time period, 3.2% beer and sniffing glue were the nearest things we had to drugs.

During my senior year, our football team was the best in the city, ranked third best in the state, and it was the last undefeated team our school ever had. Most of the football players went to the dances on Friday nights, just to be seen in their orange and black letter jackets.

I became acquainted with a number of the officers who worked the dances, especially during my senior year. I often talked to them about taking the test for police officer when I turned 21. At the time, though, I had dreams of going to college and coming back as a football coach for my alma mater. I did return after graduation and volunteer to help the wrestling coach for two years.

After my freshman year at the University of Toledo, where I did play football, I could not find a way to pay for my sophomore year. I decided to join the Army National Guard. To this day, I feel that the six months of active duty made me a better person, and I learned more about life in general than I did during any other period in my life. Because of my own experiences, I feel that every male and female – under certain guidelines – would benefit from spending six months of active duty, serving their country.

After completing my basic training in the Army, I was assigned to the Military Police School at Fort Gordon, Georgia for the remainder of my active duty. This is when I started thinking seriously about becoming a police officer.

I finished my active duty in 1963 and headed home. I found a job at a local drug store in the east end of town, as the Assistant Hardware Department Manager. The starting salary at this position was $1.25 an hour. Though I enjoyed the work, I knew this was not what I wanted to do for the rest of my life.

That same year, I took the test for police officer for the city and finished at number 47 out of 500 candidates who were vying for the position. When it came time for my interview, I was rejected, due to my weight. I was told that I would be kept on the list for future classes, and it was suggested that I lose some weight if I was really interested in joining the force. In those days, they had very tough standards for minimum height and weight, but nothing concrete for maximum weight, only that it had to be proportionate to the height. Well, mine wasn't; I was quite heavy at the time.

Another acquaintance of mine – a high school class-mate and fellow wrestler – had the same problem with his weight. We discussed our dilemma and decided if the City was going to give us another chance to lose the weight and we truly wanted to become police officers, then we better make an effort to slim down. Our plan was to accomplish this together. We were both members of the Downtown YMCA and, since we both worked the afternoon shift, we planned to meet at the "Y" in the morning.

At least four days a week, we lifted weights, ran, swam, and took a steam bath. My friend worked every night until 11:00 p.m. and I worked until 9:30 p.m., so we would meet every night at 11:30 p.m. at one of the parks in the west part of the city, as we both lived in that part of town. We would do a few exercises each night and then run a mile or two.

He beat me racing every night, except one, when I

ran through the golf course and stepped on a snake. There was no way anyone could have caught me that night. I arrived back at the cars and waited for what seemed an eternity – and was probably just a few seconds – before he caught up to me. I told him it was the last time I would run through that park at night. From that night on, we met at one of the new high schools in the west end of the city and did our nightly workout on the track behind the school building.

In October of 1964, he received the call again for the job and was accepted this time. He started as a Clerk in the police Records Section until the names on the remaining list were exhausted. I knew then that I had to continue to lose weight, as I definitely would have at least another interview before taking the test again. So, I continued to run and work out each day.

In the beginning of December, 1964, I received the phone call I had been waiting for and scheduled an interview with the Chief of Police and members of the Civil Service Board for the City. I felt I did well on the interview, but did not hear anything for a few days. Then came the call to report to the city doctor for a physical. I wanted to make sure I was at the lowest weight possible, as I really wanted the job. I had heard of stories where applicants, who were just under the minimum height requirement, had their physicals scheduled the first thing in the morning, as you are at your maximum height upon awakening. I knew of at least two applicants for the job, who spent the money to have an ambulance take them from their bed at home to the entrance of the doctor's office, where all they did was walk in and get measured immediately for their height. There were others that were under the minimum weight and would eat a whole stalk – not a bunch – of bananas the night before or just before getting weighed. There was a place in the city that also served what they called "Moron Malts," which were made in buckets, like the ones they serve popcorn in at the movie theatres, and some of these guys would also drink one of these before going to get weighed.

Me, I was different. I had to go in at the lowest weight I could. I went to see my family doctor and told him I had my physical scheduled the next morning. He knew that the only problem I would have with the physical was my weight, as I was otherwise in good condition. He gave me a double water shot at the office and some water pills to take before I went to bed that night. Well, needless to say, I spent the rest of that afternoon and night in the bathroom getting rid of all the excess water in my system.

My physical with the city doctor was scheduled for 8:00 a.m. I went through all the usual steps for the physical, but noticed that between them, the doctor and nurse had taken my blood pressure five or six times. The doctor completed his examination and said to me, "I can pass you on your weight of 224 pounds – hadn't weighed that since basic training – and the rest of the physical, but I cannot get a blood pressure on you."

I explained to him what I had done to get to the lowest weight that morning and he suggested that I come back after lunch and they would take my blood pressure again. If it was normal at that time, he would forward everything to the Chief that afternoon. I left his office and called my doctor and informed him of what happened. He told me not be too concerned, but to just go have a lunch of highly-seasoned food and that would bring my blood pressure up.

I went to a place in downtown Toledo that served the best chili mac around. I ordered one with a side order of tamales. I must have consumed at least three cokes and three glasses of water, while sweating profusely. About an hour and a half later, I went back to the city doctor's office and had the nurse take my blood pressure. The nurse smiled and said it was much better and she would tell the doctor, who would then forward the results to the Chief and Civil Service Board.

I did not hear anything until January 15, 1965, just about a month later. I was working at the drug store that day, after we had fifteen inches of snow dumped on us. We had lost power for most of the day, but had not closed the store. We shoveled the sidewalk to keep the entrance clear so we could greet customers at the doorway and then assist them through the store with the aid of flashlights. We then would guide them to the checkout where the items were rung up. This had to be done with the hand crank on the side of the cash register, due to the loss of power. The customers were then given a hand-written receipt – bet this would not happen in too many places in today's world. The power finally came on around 7:30 p.m.

At 8:30 p.m., I received a page for an outside phone call. It was my mother and she stated that a police officer had just dropped off an envelope addressed to me. I asked her if he had said anything about what it was all about and she told me no. I asked her if she could tell me what it said. She said that she had promised the officer that she would not open it, but would wait until I opened the letter myself. I explained to the manager exactly what had occurred at home and asked if I could leave early. He told me that it was fine to leave and to be sure and keep him informed of what was going on.

I had a 1961 Chevrolet Corvair at the time, and it took me over an hour and a half to get home through the snow that night. Normally, the commute would be 30 to 35 minutes. All the way home, all I could imagine was that I had received a letter of rejection, as they were scheduling another police test within the next couple of weeks.

As I took the envelope from my mother's hand, I tried to read her face for a reaction, but was unable to do so. I ripped the envelope open and the first word I read on the letter was "Congratulations." I was elated. The letter was signed by the Safety Director and Chief of Police of the City and stated that I was being hired as a Police Officer Trainee and that I should report to work at 8:00 a.m. on January 18th. I would then be assigned to the Traffic Bureau until the next police class started. The 18th was only three days away. I called my manager the first thing on Saturday morning and told him I would like to continue to work for him as long as I could. He said he was sure we could work something out.

I reported to work on Monday, January 18, 1965, as a Police Officer Trainee, actually a Traffic Bureau clerk. This was the start of my career of thirty-four-plus years with the Toledo Police Department. My starting pay was $6,450.00 a year and I thought that was all the money in the world.

The Boat Ride

*W*hile in the Academy, I purchased a boat, for no other reason than I had the money and felt I might as well buy one. It was a 16-foot Trojan with a teakwood deck and a 75-horsepower Evinrude outboard motor.

Everybody told me that it was a beautiful boat. I thought I would be able to go fishing quite often, but soon learned that this was the wrong kind of boat for fishing, as it was all enclosed, except for the front and rear seating areas.

One Sunday afternoon, William Bargania, a classmate in the police academy, and his friend and I, decided that we would cruise that afternoon. This was about three weeks after the famous Palm Sunday tornado. I had never owned or operated a boat as powerful as this one. My only experience was with a small aluminum boat with, at most, a 10-horsepower outboard motor on it.

We were able to get the boat in the water with ease and, while cruising the bay area, we decided to take a trip down to the Sturgeon Club on Whitewater Drive to have a sandwich and refreshments. As we were approaching the dock, I attempted to put the boat in neutral, in order to coast up to the dock area; but I mistakenly put it full throttle heading right for the dock. People on the dock actually jumped off, as they thought I was going to run into the dock.

I managed to turn it around, so we could head away from the dock and get slowly turned around. This time, we made it to the dock all right. We sure received a lot of dirty looks and comments from people as we pulled in. We had a sandwich and refreshments and decided to hit the bay and cruise for a while.

We were zipping up and down the bay at 28-mph when we hit something on the right front part of the boat, which we later discovered was a part of a telephone pole from the tornado. Water started gushing in and I yelled to Bill to put his foot on the hole to keep the water from coming in. Needless to say, that did not work too well.

The water was up to our waists now. Bill and his friend jumped out of the boat and were holding onto the seat cushions. The motor had stalled out and I had to reach under water to locate the ignition, so I could try to start the engine.

At that point, I decided it was time to get the hell out. William's friend kept yelling that he could not swim. We tried to keep him cool and told him not to worry, all the while attempting to convince him to hold onto the boat, as it was made of wood and would not sink. That was the wrong thing to say, because, just as the words came out of our mouths, the boat disappeared under water. The expression on his face was that of horror. Thank God, the boat reappeared in a few seconds. We then held onto the boat and screamed for help. That didn't work. Bill and I remembered we had our police whistles with us, so we started blowing on them.

Finally, a family came along in a boat. They assisted us in moving my boat over to a small island. The family took William's friend into their boat and said they would contact the Coast Guard. Bill and I stayed with the boat on the little island. We spent about fifteen minutes gathering all the seat cushions and other items from the lake. We felt like we were on "Gilligan's Island" while we waited for the Coast Guard to return for us.

There we sat, leaning up against the boat, waiting for the Coast Guard. To pass the time, we started throwing stones at the seagulls. Boy, is that the wrong thing to do. Within five minutes they were swarming down on us. One hit me in the head with its beak, drawing blood – I mean a lot of blood. It was streaming down my face when the Coast Guard arrived. They treated my head wound and advised me to get a tetanus shot as soon as I could.

The Coast Guard put us on board ship and towed the boat into Harrison Marina on Summit Street. They informed me at the marina that, if they started work on the engine within 24 hours, it could probably be saved. I told them to get started as soon as they could. As we walked out of the marina towards our car, water squishing out of our shoes every step of the way, a police cruiser was sitting there, waiting to take our report. After they found out who we were, they had a real good laugh.

Of course, by the next morning, the entire department knew about the two rookies in the academy sinking a 32-foot boat. See how the size of the boat grew overnight. Not long after the engine was repaired and the hole in the boat was fixed, there was a large "For Sale" sign on the boat.

The Armband Meant Nothing

One night in late May of 1965, two of my classmates from the academy and I decided we needed a night out. I lived in west Toledo and Bill and Ethan lived in north Toledo. We decided to patronize a few of the businesses in north Toledo on this particular night.

Our only means of identification with the City of Toledo Police Department were canvas armbands that read "Toledo Police Academy". We were instructed that these were to be worn when we were assigned any special duty, such as traffic assignments, etc. We first wore them when we were activated for traffic and special duties after the Palm Sunday tornado in 1965.

We started out at one of the establishments that specialized in pizza and spaghetti and also had a nice lounge area. We had a very good pizza and a couple of beers at this location and then decided to stop by Samuels Bar and have a drink.

Back then, Samuels Bar was known as a pretty tough place. A lot of "hoods" supposedly hung out there. I had never been to many places outside of the west end, so I really did not know. When I mentioned the supposed toughness that I had heard of regarding this bar, my classmates just shrugged it off. They informed me that they were from the north end, had been at this place several times, and never experienced any problems.

When we arrived, the place was jam-packed with people and there were at least 25 to 30 motorcycles parked in the front. The place was really rocking with music playing on the jukebox. We found a small table in a corner that wasn't occupied and, when the barmaid approached us, we all ordered a beer to drink. The noise and music was so deafening, we almost had to yell at each other across the table to be heard.

The song "Can't Get No Satisfaction" was blaring from the jukebox. Everyone was singing along to the music, which added to the clamor in the establishment. All of a sudden, there was a big commotion in the middle of the floor and we could see that a fight had broken out amongst a group of people. We heard someone yell to call the police and, within seconds, we could hear sirens in the background, so we assumed they were headed our way.

Ethan, who stood only about 5'8" and weighed about 150 pounds, decided he was going to break up the fight. We tried to convince him that we, as probationary patrol-men, were not supposed to be in places like this. He insisted that he try and break up the fight. He got up, removed his armband from his pocket, and headed for the melee in the middle of the floor.

Bill and I stood up and were going to follow him, just as he got in the middle of the brawl. We watched as he was waving his armband and yelling, "Break it up, I'm a Toledo Police Officer."

Next thing we knew, he was being picked up and thrown through the plate glass window at the front of the bar. Bill and I turned around quickly and vacated the premises via the rear door. We knew now that we would really be in a heap of trouble if the Commanders of the police academy got word of this night out.

We went around to the front of the building and Ethan was just getting up off the ground. He had a few cuts on his arms and a small one on the right side of his forehead.

We decided the best thing was to get away from that place and go home where we belonged. The next day in the academy, Ethan did not look too worse for wear. A few of our classmates asked him what happened, and he told them he had walked into the bathroom door at home during the night.

That was the last time I was ever in that bar and, I assume, the last time for Bill and Ethan too.

The Bear Got the Best of It

I remember the officers working in the Traffic Bureau telling me a story about an officer named Jim "Steer" Milner. The tale revolved around a circus that had a "boxing" bear and had came to town three or four years before that. They offered $500.00 to anyone who could last through three, two-minute rounds with the bear. The bear was housed in a building just off an alley behind the police service station on Spielbush.

When one of the officers told Steer about the bear being housed near the service station, he decided to go over and check it out. After observing the bear, it did not seem to him to be that big, so Steer decided that he would sign up for the bout with the bear. Now Steer was a pretty big fellow, about 6'3" and weighing around 240 pounds He was also in great shape, as he had done some boxing in his past.

I don't remember if the story claimed that he lasted the three rounds or not. I do remember talking to Steer a few years later and he told me that, when he entered the ring and the bear stood on its hind legs, it was about seven feet tall. Steer said he hit that bear as hard as he could right in the snout and the bear just shook its head. He proceeded to hit him a few more times before the bear took a swing at him, hitting him on the shoulder. Steer told me that, when the bear hit him, it knocked him across the ring. He told me he got up and hit the bear a few more times and it happened again. Steer admitted that he, not the bear, got the worst of it. I never did hear if Steer got the $500.00 or not.

While on the subject of Steer Milner, there was a story a few years later that I remember vividly, because I was involved in this one. I was working West Toledo and Steer was working with another officer in a Traffic Car. The other officer was driving. We were in a chase involving a motorcycle on Telegraph Road from Laskey Road, going towards the state line. We were behind the motorcycle and couldn't catch him, so the Traffic Car went around us and pulled alongside the cycle. Steer leaned out the window and grabbed the guy by the back of the neck and lifted him right off the cycle. The cycle kept going off into a field. We pulled up alongside the traffic car and, literally, took him out of Steer's hands.

The suspect could not believe what had transpired; as a matter of fact, it was quite astonishing to us, too. I would have had trouble believing this story if I had not seen it myself. Steer acted as though it was just another routine incident.

First Assignment

*A*fter graduating from the Police Academy, my first assignment was on the midnight shift. I had never worked past 10 p.m. in my life. My first night on the street, I was assigned to Unit 12, a paddy wagon in the inner city. The Officer I worked with that night was Dan Dierterduck, a veteran of seven or eight years. We had 29 calls for service and it was one helluva night.

When we hit on, we stopped at Frisch's Drive-In Restaurant at Monroe & Bancroft. This was back when they still had carhops who brought a tray to set on your window, and your coffee was served in china cups. Our coffee had just arrived, when we received a call regarding a disturbance – man stabbed – at Brewster's Bar on Nebraska near Westwood. Dan was driving that night and he backed the wagon out of the parking space with coffee, cups, and tray flying, as he turned on the lights and siren and sped off.

Upon our arrival, we entered the bar and observed a number of persons pointing and yelling at a white male with a large knife in one hand and a pool stick in the other. They were all shouting that he was the person responsible for the stabbing. We then observed another male laying on the pool table, bleeding profusely from a wound in his abdomen. After calling for an ambulance, we were able to convince the suspect to drop the knife and pool stick. As he dropped the two weapons, we quickly cuffed him and placed him in the rear of the paddy wagon.

Meanwhile, an ambulance arrived and transported the victim to Mercy Hospital. The Detectives were called and we were instructed to bring the suspect to the Detective Bureau for questioning. In those days, the Detectives on the night shift were so busy that they normally did not come to the scene.

Because Dan was driving, I had to ride in the rear of the wagon with the suspect. This being my first night and first felony arrest, I was nervous as hell. The suspect sat across from me at the front of the rear compartment of the wagon and I sat near the back. I had one hand on my revolver in the holster and the other on my nightstick, all the way downtown, not taking my eyes off of him the entire time. Keep in mind that he was cuffed with his hands behind him all the while.

The rest of the night was mostly family disputes and suspicious persons and cars – nothing very serious. I went home and was in bed by 7 a.m. and slept straight through until 8:30 p.m. the next night, just in time to get up and get ready for work. That second night, I worked with Chad Dierterduck, Dan's brother. We worked Unit 19 in West Toledo and did not receive an assignment for service all night long. What a difference!

First Beat Assignment

*A*fter the first two nights, I was assigned a lot of foot patrol. Little did I know, at the time, that walking a beat was one of the best duties! Back then there were no portable radios, so you checked in with the dispatch officer by calling on the police phone. These were located on corners throughout the city and they had a special key to open them. Inside was a phone that went directly to the "box" in the dispatcher's office. You were not allowed to hit the same box twice in a row. You were assigned to hit on the hour, fifteen minutes after, a half-hour or forty-five minutes after the hour. You could not hit the box any sooner than ten minutes before or ten minutes after your designated time.

If you failed to make your call during the designated times, the radio dispatcher then would put out a broadcast in an attempt to locate the officer in question.

One instance, I remember very well, occurred one morning in July of 1965, at approximately 6:30 a.m. I was working the 11 to 7 shift and had been walking the beat in the downtown area. While I was standing at the corner of Adams and Huron, waiting to inform the dispatcher by phone that my assignment was complete for the night, Officer John Carpeto was at the corner of Adams and Superior, one block east of my location.

The sun had just come up and it was a beautiful morning. We were both watching a worker cleaning windows, up on the sixth floor of Latrelle's. He had just finished one window and was moving to the next. He stepped onto the ledge of the next window and reached out to attach his safety belt and clip it in place. He slipped and fell, as he was reaching out with the snap.

We watched him tumble through the air turning over and over and, when he landed on the sidewalk, he landed feet first.

John and I ran over to him and he was a crumbled mess. The last words out of his mouth were, "Help me." When he landed on his feet, his legs were shoved right up through his body through his shoulders and blood was everywhere. I had to run to the corner and call for an ambulance on the "box", as we did not have portable radios back then.

It was a real mess. I can still, till this day, see him tumbling through the air and knowing there was nothing I could do to help him.

Handling Domestic Disturbances

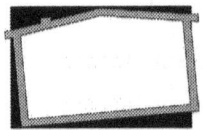

I filled in on some of the inner city crews when I first became an officer. The crews assigned to the inner city were racially mixed. It was a different experience seeing how the people believed and respected the policemen who worked in their area. The older officers in this area were believed in and respected by the people in their districts. The officers ran their territory a little different than what we had been taught in the Police Academy.

When called to a disturbance–what today is called a domestic disturbance–one way that the older officers would settle the disturbance would be to get everyone quieted down and then ask them if they were married. If they answered, "Yes, we are married," he would then respond that that was the problem. He would tell them if they wanted to solve the problem immediately, they would have to be divorced. Then he would have them both stand up and place their right hands on his badge.

The Officer would then say to them, after raising his right hand in the air, "By the power vested in me by the grand State of Ohio here in Lucas County, I now claim that (*he would state their names*) are now divorced." They would actually thank the crew as the Officers left, and everything would be peaceful for a few days. If the answer was that the couple were not married or had been divorced earlier, then they were told that they would have to get married. The officer would then marry the couple by placing their hands on the officer's badge and he would, by the power vested in him by the State of Ohio, marry the couple.

Once again, problem solved, and this, I guess, was one of the old ways of doing Community Policing. It was one of the easiest ways to settle domestic disputes back then. It hardly took any time and everyone thought the policemen were the greatest.

First Cadaver

One of the things you never forget on the job is your first dead body. It remains vividly in your mind for the rest of your life. My first was during the winter months of 1966; I can remember we were wearing our "Reefers". These were weighty, long coats, falling beyond our fingertips and made out of a heavy cloth-type material.

I was working with Jack Janowicki on the day shift and had just "hit on" with the dispatcher, who gave us a call to meet the apartment manager and check the safety of one of the occupants at a building on 15th Street, just off of Adams. When we arrived, the building manager approached us and stated: "I think something is wrong in unit #5. There is a strong odor coming from the apartment and I've heard water running in there for the last few days." As we entered the building, the smell was enough to make you gag and cause your eyes to burn.

The apartment manager continued, "I thought the smell was from a dead rat or something in the basement, until I seen the water seeping through the floor." Well, that was our first clue that there was something amiss in apartment #5.

The manager did not have a key, so we proceeded to break down the door. Now, these apartments were not luxury jobs, by any means. The door was very flimsy and all it took was a good shoulder to pop it right open. The smell that hit me when I went through was absolutely gut wrenching and then I saw the body. It was lying across the bed on its back and, at first, I thought it was a black male, as most of the body was black.

The body looked like it was covered with white rice, only the rice was moving. The maggots were all over his head and upper torso. The cadaver had blown up to almost twice the size of a normal person. With that I put my hand over my mouth and ran outside and tossed my cookies. We called for the coroner and an ambulance via the radio in the wagon.

When Runner Ambulance arrived, they had a good time laughing, because I was still having the dry heaves. Of course it was a lot easier for them, as they wore masks to cover their faces. They came in and brought a large rubber, zippered bag. They laid it down on the bed, hoisted the body, and placed it on top of the bag. As they did, all the innards of the body burst open and the skin cracked, as the fluids ran into the bag.

The smell was now twice as bad as before. I went outside and did it again. This time I had a real problem getting myself under control. As we wrapped up the paper work and were about to pull away, Jack said, "Let's go to Elmer's Diner and have some breakfast, some really snotty-type scrambled eggs with lots of catsup on them." That did it for me and, for the third time, I jumped out of the wagon and dry heaved again for about fifteen minutes, all the while calling Jack every name in the book. Of course he was laughing his ass off.

For a week straight, as soon as I was off duty, I took my "reefer" to the one-hour cleaners to try and get the smell out.

Where's My Partner?

*A*nother night, I was working with Darryl and it was around 2:30 in the morning. We were on 15th street approaching Madison Avenue, when the dispatcher put out a description of a red Ford Fairlane involved in an armed robbery on Reynolds Road, a few minutes prior.

Well, Reynolds Road was a long way from Madison Avenue and not too much was thought of it at first. As we approached the stop sign on Fifteenth at Madison, a red Ford Fairlane went by westbound on Madison Avenue, which was a one-way street.

The description had included a white male and female in the car and this vehicle fit the description. I was driving, so I turned left from Fifteenth Street onto Madison and started following the vehicle. I assumed Darryl was paying attention, while I was watching the vehicle in question and talking. I asked Darryl, "What do you think, should we stop them?" Darryl grunted, "Yeah, go ahead."

As we approached Mercy Hospital, I turned on the overhead flashing light and the car pulled over to the left curb in front of the hospital. The driver exited the vehicle somewhat hurriedly and I exited the driver's side of our wagon at the same time. I had removed my revolver as I exited the paddy wagon and had it trained on the suspect, while shielding myself with the open door of our police vehicle. I instructed the suspect to put his hands on top of the car and step back. He did just as he was told.

I told Darryl, "Go up and get the keys out of the car and remove the passenger." No response from Darryl, so I repeated myself, but still nothing. At that point, I glanced over to the passenger seat in the wagon and, as I did, the suspect jumped back in his car and took off. Darryl was still sitting in the passenger seat writing – as I discovered later – his Amway order.

The vehicle fled west towards Collingwood, turned left, and then turned left again at Jefferson. There was no way the wagon would be able to keep up with the car. I broadcasted the vehicle description immediately and requested assistance from other crews. The chase ended in the old middle grounds near the Maumee River with an altercation and shots being fired by another crew. Officer Bob Kandrick was the officer who finally apprehended the suspects. Unbeknownst to the Command, Bob carried two revolvers on him when he worked. He emptied the one and then used his off-duty gun to complete the apprehension.

Another unusual story, while I was working Unit 20, involved another cadaver. We were sent to the lower apartment in a building located in the 400 block of West Bancroft. On arrival, an elderly man greeted us and told us he thought his wife needed medical assistance. He motioned us into the living room.

As we walked in, we could see there was an elderly lady lying on the floor next to the couch. We assumed that she was dead, as her right arm, from the elbow up, was sticking straight up in the air. We called for the rescue squad and proceeded to question the gentleman.

He told us that his wife had fallen off the couch on Sunday – this was Wednesday – and that he had sat there on the couch, ever since, holding her hand and talking to her. He said she didn't answer him, but he knew she hadn't been feeling well lately, so he decided that she felt too ill to talk. It was a sad story, knowing that these two people were all that each other had.

The Rescue Squad arrived and went through the formalities and pronounced her dead. We never did tell the gentleman that she had been dead for some time. We let him believe that she died that morning.

Strong Arms of Law Lift Cruiser

On February 9, 1966, I was working the 7 to 3 shift on Unit 20, the paddy wagon. It started out on the quiet side, with nothing much happening, aside from a few malicious destruction reports that had occurred on our district during the night. Around 11:00 a.m., we were dispatched to Scott High School on a wagon call for an unruly juvenile. I drove and Jack was in the passenger seat, taking reports for the day. I pulled behind Scott High School and approached the rear of the building.

Many buildings, houses and other structures were still being heated by burning coal. There were large storage areas underground for the coal at several of the buildings, which was the case in the rear of the Scott's High School property. Access to these storage areas was accomplished by lifting a manhole cover, so the coal could be dumped in the storage areas for future use.

As I approached the rear of the building, I must have hit one of the covers just right because, as I drove over it, the cover popped out and the right front wheel of our paddy wagon fell into the hole. I tried backing the paddy wagon out of the hole, but the rear wheels just spun. We notified the dispatcher of our predicament and asked him to send a tow truck to remove us from the hole. A Sergeant and an Accident Investigation Unit also had to respond to the scene. A reporter from the Toledo Blade newspaper had monitored our call and just happened to be in the vicinity and also responded.

Meanwhile, with the arrival of the Sergeant and Accident Investigation Unit, we had my partner, Jack get behind the wheel of the paddy wagon, as he was the smallest of the bunch. The rest of us grabbed whatever we could get our hands on near the right front of the paddy wagon and, on the count of three, lifted the vehicle. At the same time, Jack put the paddy wagon in reverse and was able to back out of the coal chute.

Of course, as we were lifting the wagon out of the coal chute, the reporter from the newspaper was taking pictures of the incident. The next morning there was a 5"x 5" picture on the front page of the second section of the newspaper that showed the four officers lifting the vehicle out of the coal chute. The words above the picture read "Strong Arms of Law Free Cruiser From Chute." Just a little embarrassing, and it makes you think, where are they when you really want a reporter for a story? For quite some time after this incident, I received a lot of ribbing from fellow officers.

Wrong Way to Search
A Burning Building

Jack and I were working on the midnight shift one rather warm spring evening in 1966. It was 3:30 a.m. in the morning and it was a rather quiet night. We were traveling west on Monroe Street towards Collingwood Avenue and, as we passed 15th Street, we observed smoke billowing from the windows on the first floor of a large apartment building on 15th Street.

I was driving and 15th street is a one-way street southbound, but I turned north, going the wrong way on the one-way street towards the apartment building. When we pulled up in front of the building you could feel the heat of the fire coming from the building. Jack headed for the building and, before I got out of the wagon, I notified the dispatcher by radio that we needed the fire department as we had a building on fire at this location and we were entering the building to search for any victims.

We then headed for the apartment. Remember, at this time, we did not have portable radios. The apartment that the smoke and fire was coming from was on the left side of the building as you entered. Jack entered the apartment ahead of me. I lost sight of him as soon as he walked into the apartment. I entered behind him and started searching the rooms.

Before I knew it, I was coughing and hacking. My eyes were burning and I could hardly breathe. I continued to search the rooms as best I could until I could not take the heat and smoke any longer. I attempted to find my way out and, as I did, I tripped over something, as I headed for the light and what I thought was the entrance to the apartment. I almost landed on the floor of the apartment and, as I tripped, my partner screamed that I had kicked him. It was he whom I had tripped over. He was on his hands and knees crawling around searching the rooms... little did I know that this *was* the way to search a burning building, one thing we were never taught in the academy. We were unable to find any victims in the apartment.

As we exited the apartment, the firemen were arriving at the scene. We informed them that we had found no victims in the apartment. They put on all of their equipment and entered the building and proceeded to extinguish the fire in the kitchen.

It was later discovered that the tenants had left their apartment, apparently forgetting about the items they had cooking on the stove. Not only was there extensive smoke damage done to the apartment, but fire damage to the walls and ceiling of the kitchen.

After the fire was put out, the firemen treated me for smoke inhalation by applying oxygen at the scene and then sent me to Mercy Hospital. That was the last time I searched a building in that manner. An important lesson learned. When we had a fire on our district and the same firemen were dispatched, they always asked me if I would like to search the building for them.

Saving A Fireman

I was working the day shift with Jack in the summer of 1966. We were dispatched to Jefferson and Huron for an accident with a fire truck involved and were told to step it up, as there were several injuries involved. Upon arrival, we found the truck embedded in the building on the southeast corner. There were a number of firemen injured and one was still on the fire truck, which was halfway into the building. We were instructed to assist in removing him.

We worked right alongside some of the firemen, as we had to use extreme care in extracting him, which involved removing bricks from the building to reach him. It seemed like an eternity, but later we learned that it actually had been only a few minutes. Back in those days, Officers working the paddy wagons were often called to make an ambulance run. Usually, they were not critical, emergency-type situations. Each wagon was equipped with a portable stretcher that folded. When unfolded it could handle someone around 6'4" and, maybe, 250 pounds.

The fireman was covered with blood and bleeding profusely. We were very cautious moving him onto the stretcher, which we had placed on top of the fire truck. With the assistance of a few more firemen and police officers, we were able to lift him down over the fire truck and then load him and the stretcher into the back of the paddy wagon. Everyone was screaming at us to get moving. Jack rode in the back, with a few firemen, and I drove with lights and sirens going full blast. We headed for the closest facility, which was Mercy Hospital. The dispatcher had notified the hospital and they were outside the emergency entrance waiting with a gurney. They took over from there.

We found out later that the injured fireman's name was Jack Kendry. Jack was a well-known athlete from Toledo and was still active in sports in the city. For the next few months, every time we stopped at a firehouse, we would inquire about his progress and were always told that his condition was improving. Seven or eight months after the accident, Jack came to our roll call to personally thank all the crews for their efforts that day and he made special mention of me and my partner, Jack. He stated that, if it had not been for our actions that day, he might not be alive.

We took pride in our involvement in the rescue. It is one of the first times I can recall helping someone who may have died if we hadn't been there.

What A Battle

*O*ne of the toughest scuffles I was ever involved in was with a black male with the name of Marvin Trooner. Marv was around 5'10" tall and weighed about 250 pounds, but was solid as a rock. Marv had a drinking problem, though he had a decent job and his wife was a schoolteacher. I was working with Jack in the winter of 1966 and we were dispatched to pick up a prisoner at Mercy Hospital Emergency Room.

It was Marvin. He had been drinking with some of his friends and they had bet him $20.00 that he could not drink a bottle of Vodka straight down. Well, Marvin did it and ended up getting arrested for being drunk and disorderly. He was then taken to Mercy Hospital to get his stomach pumped. He was really pissed at that point, because his friends had taken off without honoring their bet.

Marvin was usually peaceful but, when he got nasty, you had your hands full. As we walked out the door of the emergency room, I recall that it was a very cold day. Jack had him by one arm and I had the other. When he felt the blast of cold air, Marvin went berserk. He threw Jack up against the wall knocking him, not out cold, but making him woozy enough to prevent him from getting up right away. When you work a wagon, you always wear gloves and I had purchased a pair of leather gloves that had powdered lead in the knuckles.

As Jack went up against the wall, Marvin was screaming and acting like a maniac. I never let go of his arm but wound up and backhanded him right across the nose. Well it looked like his nose was moved over about two inches on his face and blood was flying everywhere. He went down and I went down with him. We wrestled around on the ground and snow until I finally managed to get the cuffs on him. Of course, now I was covered with blood and Jack was still woozy against the building. After I saw what I had done to Marvin's eye and nose, with just a backhand, I never again wore those gloves.

Jack recovered enough to get up, and Marvin decided to come along peacefully. The only problem was that we had to take him back into the emergency room. They put nine stitches over his right eye and a few around his nose.

We didn't see Marvin for a few months until, one day, we were at the State Mental Hospital on another wagon run. Marvin was a patient there but, as a trustee, he had ground privileges. He came walking up to me, looked me in the eye, pointed to the scar over his eye and said, "You're the one who did that to me, aren't you officer?" I answered, "Yes, Marvin, I did that to you; do you remember how it happened?" He said, "No sir, and I want to apologize for being so bad that day. I really am sorry about it, Officer."

I told Marvin that it was okay. We talked for a few minutes and he told me how he was going to be all right when he got out. We didn't see Marvin very much after that. I heard he cut down on his drinking; but he died around fifty-seven years of age.

In The Hole

$\mathcal{D}$arryl, a fellow police officer and classmate, who attended the Academy with me, bought a house on Warren Street off of Bancroft. It was a big, three-story house, located in the inner city. Most of the old houses in that vicinity were large in size. The house had a roomy four-car garage in the back end of the structure. The driveway was not paved, nor was the floor of the garage.

Darryl had an old Volkswagen bus that he drove as his family car. He decided that he wanted to work on the Volkswagen himself and it would be nice to have a pit in the garage. He dug out a large pit and, when he wanted to make repairs on the VW, he would just pull the bus over the hole and then climb into the pit to work on the vehicle. Three or four months later, he bought a motor-cycle, with the thought that he would get better gas mileage and his wife could use the Volkswagen bus to transport their children.

Shortly after he bought the motorcycle, we were working the three-to-eleven shift. One particular shift, he came into work looking like he had been through a war, with cuts and bruises all over his arms and face. I asked, "What in the hell happened to you?" He explained that his wife had used the VW and parked it in a different section of the garage. When Darryl arrived home after work the previous night, he roared up the drive into the garage, right into the pit. He told me he had to leave the cycle in the pit, as he could not get it out by himself.

After work, five or six of us went over and helped him get the cycle out of the pit and had a good laugh over it. I think he sold the motorcycle shortly after that.

Fast Wagon ~ Men's Jail

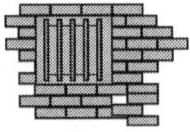

I was working day shift with Darryl when we received a call for a "fast wagon" in the men's jail in the Safety Building. A fast wagon meant that everyone in service available to take a call should respond, as there was a police officer in trouble. At the time, we housed our own prisoners, and the men's jail was on the 5th floor.

We were not very far away, so we responded very quickly. Unit #1, Officers Bill Daumgarder and Bob Wast were already there. We immediately went to the 5th floor and discovered they had everything under control by this time.

Someone explained that one of the prisoners, whose last name was Carter, had reached through his cell window and had worked loose a part of the bar on the window. The bars on the windows were rather fancy and the iron on the bars was shaped like fig leaves, one of which he had removed. When Officer Tim Hale, the jailer, took him to the shower area, Carter attacked Officer Hale with this leaf-shaped piece of iron. The room where this occurred was approximately twelve-by-twelve feet. It looked like they had slaughtered a hog in there, as there was blood covering all the walls, ceiling and floor.

Sergeant Portnoy was the command officer in charge of the scene at the time and he told Daumgarder, Wast, Darryl and myself to transfer this subject to a "blind cell" – a type of solitary confinement.

I was holding onto one of the prisoner's arms, as we were transferring him into the cell. With blood on the soles of my shoes, I slipped on the wet floor, tripped, and fell. The subject, Carter, and I fell to the floor and, as we went down, I landed on his chest. He had to be treated at the hospital for broken ribs and other injuries.

We learned later that the prisoner had been picked up on Cherry Street near Huron, driving a vehicle with Michigan plates. I don't know what the circumstances were or why he was initially stopped; but, when they searched the trunk, they found body parts in boxes. In one, they found the entire torso and a few others had arms and legs in them. I guess the one that really got to everybody was the box that had a whole head in it.

I don't recall exactly what happened to Carter after this, but I do know Tim Hale was never the same again. He became hard of hearing, had severe headaches and various other problems. He had to take an early disability retirement.

Riot at the Workhouse

*W*e were working the 11 to 7 shift and had stopped to get something to eat. As soon as we placed our food order, we were told to call the dispatcher by phone. We went to the nearest call box and were told we had to meet the Lieutenant at Monroe & Erie Streets and we would be out of service.

When we reached Monroe and Erie, five other police cars had already arrived and three more showed up, plus the Lieutenant and Sergeant. We were told that we were going to the workhouse in Whitehouse, Ohio, where prisoners were sentenced on misdemeanor charges. It was located about 15 miles from downtown Toledo. We were informed that they were having a large disturbance involving the inmates.

We started out the Anthony Wayne Trail in single file, going the speed limit and stopping for all traffic lights and traffic signs. As we approached the City limits, the dispatcher told us to step it up, as the situation was getting worse.

We turned on our lights and sirens and it must have looked pretty impressive with nine black and white police cars and a paddy wagon, all in line with their lights and sirens on, crashing all the red lights.

When we arrived, we were told to put our riot helmets on and carry our gas masks, in case they were needed. We entered one of the buildings and started up the stairs, aware that most of the lights in the building had been broken out.

On the stairway, the Lieutenant used a bullhorn to instruct everyone upstairs to come out one by one with their hands over their heads. The reply from the inmates was not what we wanted. They started throwing anything they could get their hands on down the stairs at us – I mean, bed frames, tables, and all that good stuff. We decided to retreat a little down the steps and to the outside to regroup.

After a discussion outside, it was decided to use tear gas. We all put on our gas masks and the Lieutenant fired four rounds of tear gas into their area. It wasn't long before they decided to see things our way.

We made them strip down to their shorts before they came out and we then searched each individual. While checking the rear of one individual's shorts, I found a string around his waist. I had him drop his shorts and get up against the wall, with his hands on the wall and his legs spread. As he did this, a small .22 caliber derringer swung out from under his scrotum. This became an additional charge we were able to put on him.

When we finally removed everyone and were able to go upstairs, we were shocked at the amount of home-made weapons we found. The place looked like a bomb went off in the area.

Most of the inmates involved were transferred to other facilities. We – the wagon – transported five of the inmates back downtown for additional charges and questioning.

The Gold Badge Shineth

One of the most memorable times I had during my career was a summer night in 1966. I was working Unit 20, the downtown area wagon, and had received a call for a Malicious Destruction (known now as Criminal Damage) report at the Mirror Bar on Madison at 16th street. These types of calls were taken as in-service calls, which meant that one officer would stay with the vehicle while the other took the report and, if you received a higher priority call before you finished this report, you were to take the higher priority call first.

Some unknown suspect had thrown a beer bottle through the window of the Mirror Bar. My partner was in the bar taking the report, while I sat in the wagon, listening for calls. While waiting, I observed a white-colored Oldsmobile come up 16th from Adams and stop at the traffic sign at Madison, about 20 feet from where I was situated under a tree, with my vehicle lights off.

There was a female driving the vehicle and a male in the passenger seat. I could see the male had his arm around the female and he was leaning over kissing her. All at once, I saw him sit back and hit her across the face with his right hand. The car took off crossing Madison, squealing its tires. At that moment, Darryl exited the bar with the report. I watched the car pull over in front of the Hillcrest Hotel on the 16th street side, opposite Madison Avenue. I quickly told Darryl what had transpired and said, "Let's go check this out."

As I turned the corner onto 16th, the passenger exited the car and started walking towards Madison Avenue. I told Darryl to go to the Oldsmobile and check the female and see if she was all right. The male passenger was walking near the rear of the wagon on the sidewalk when I shouted to him, "Hold on a minute; I want to talk to you." This guy was about 5'9" tall and weighed about 230 pounds and was built pretty solid. He was in his late 40's or early 50's and fairly well dressed. He turned around towards me and said, "Fuck you, I don't have to talk to you kid!"

Right then, I knew that he had flunked this rookie's attitude test and I was going to have problems. I went up to him and grabbed him by the arm and started to explain what I wanted; but I never got the words out of my mouth, as he turned and swung at me. I blocked the punch with my left arm and hit him along the side of his head and he fell back towards the wagon. He came at me again and I grabbed him by the back of his sports coat and ran him face first into one of the steel light poles, ripping his coat up the back. I tore it bad enough that it was beyond repair. He swung at me one more time and, once again, I blocked it and hit him hard in the chest with my forearm, driving him backwards into the side of the wagon.

As he staggered away from the vehicle, he reached into his inside jacket pocket and out came the shiniest gold Toledo Police Sergeant's Badge that I had ever seen. The damn thing looked like it had neon lights around it. Well, at that point, I am ready to change my underwear. Here I am, one of the new kids on the street, and I just smacked a sergeant all around the street. I didn't know what to do. I told him I was very sorry for the misunderstanding and his words were, "I could have kicked your ass, kid."

Not knowing what to do, as the victim had driven away before we could talk to her, I let the Sergeant go. I later learned that this was Sergeant Bill Monphry from the Detective Bureau. At one time, he had played pro-football with the Chicago Bears.

Later that night, it started bothering me that this female could have been injured and there was no report made and I could be in a heap of trouble. I called and met my Lieutenant and told him the entire story. He told me to make out a Sergeant's report, stating exactly what happened, and he would give it to the chief, if he thought it was serious enough. I went home that day and, around 11:30 in the morning, my mother woke me to tell me the chief was on the phone. I answered the phone and he said he wanted to see me in his office at 1:00 p.m. I said I would be there.

When I arrived at the Chief's office, he asked me to come in and sit down. I sat right across from him at his desk and he asked me to retell the story, just as it happened. He had Deputy Chief Meeker typing every-thing I said as I told the story. Deputy Chief Meeker and Chief Bosch were what we now call Internal Affairs; they handled all complaints against police officers. There were no tape recorders or computers in those days, so all statements were taken and typed on manual type-writers and seven copies of the reports were made on the typewriter.

After it was all over, he said to me, "What did you think when he pulled the badge out?" I replied, "Chief, I had to go home and change my pants." The chief asked me if I checked to see if he was carrying his gun and I said, "Hell no!" That was one of the few times I saw Chief Bosch laugh.

I later learned that they charged Monphry with

intoxication, resisting arrest, conduct unbecoming, and causing a disturbance. He did 60 days suspension on these charges. Shortly after he retired, he was picked up at Churchill's for shoplifting crabmeat. I had the wagon call, but I don't think he remembered me from our first encounter, as nothing was ever said.

The Very Large Prostitute

*I*t was autumn of 1966, a clear sky with the temperature in the mid-60's, making it a nice, early, fall night. At 1:00 in the morning, we were working our usual downtown paddy wagon district when we received a call to assist the Vice Officer with an arrest at Monroe and 10th. We okayed the dispatcher and had just placed the micro-phone back on the dashboard clip when we were told to step it up as he was having trouble with a prostitute.

Keep in mind that, during this time period, we still did not have portable radios and the vice officer, Jim VanDielen, had walked the prostitute to the call box at Monroe and 10th to request the wagon. She was a real heifer, about 5'5" tall and tipping the scales at about 280 pounds – not your normal-looking prostitute.

While Officer VanDielen was on the phone at the call box, requesting a wagon for transportation to the jail, he was holding the large suspect by one arm and had the phone in the other hand. The lady of the night was all decked out and was wearing stiletto-type high heels. Just as we rounded the corner, she raised her foot in the air and stomped it down on the Officer's foot, in an attempt to break free. Between her weight and the force that she put behind it, the stiletto heel went through the Officer's shoe and into his foot. As we pulled up, the Officer let go of her arm, grabbed her by the hair and was hitting her with the phone to get her to release her foot. Officer VanDielen and the prostitute both required treatment at the hospital.

When they went to court and the prostitute received her sentence, she was also ordered by the judge to pay for the replacement of Officer VanDielen's shoes. She protested loudly about having to pay for the shoes and the Judge said to her "If you do not quiet down, I will make it two pairs of shoes that you will have to pay for."

First Real Crew

*W*hile in the Academy, two other Officers and I developed a close relationship. These Officers were John "Lurch" Connors and Julius "Jeep" Materni. In 1967, I was working the paddy wagon in the downtown area, near the inner city district, and Lurch and Jeep were working the paddy wagon in the lower north end of the downtown district. Lurch was working one shift and Jeep another in the same district, but a different shift and crew. At this time, the crews were made up of three men, so that one officer was always on a day off. You worked fours days and then had two days off. That meant you had a weekend off once every seven weeks.

After graduating from the Academy, we stayed in contact with each other and would socialize once in a while. One night we were talking over a few brewskis and decided that we would like to work together, if we could somehow swing it. Back then, the Chief made all the decisions on who worked what crew and no one else had very much input regarding the decision. We decided that we had nothing to lose, so we sat down and filled out a Sergeant's Report and addressed it to the Chief, requesting to work together as a crew on a wagon. We explained that we had no preference as to district, just that we thought we could work well together. About four months went by and we heard nothing about our request.

We were out together again one night, and decided that we should all go together and request to see the Chief and explain the situation to him. We figured we had nothing to lose and none of us were happy with the crews we were working at the time. We arrived at the Chief's office and told Barb Goating, the Chief's Secretary, that we would like to talk to the Chief, if he had a few free minutes. The three of us were still on probation for one year after graduation from the Academy, and I was still battling to keep my weight down to the weight that I started at the Academy. I had to keep that weight until I was off probation. Barb got up and walked to the Chief's door and said, "Chief, your prize steer, O.J., and two of his friends are here to see you."

We were nervous as hell because, as I said before, back in those days the Chief was "Boss" and you knew it. He told Barb to have us come into his Office. We entered and stood at attention in front of his desk and saluted. He told us to take a seat and state our business. We explained to him that we went through the Academy together and were all working wagons, either in the downtown area or near the downtown area, and none of us were happy on the crews we were working. We further explained that we really did not care where we worked, but would prefer a district in the inner-city area.

We had heard from other Officers that the downtown and near downtown districts were the Chief's favorite and special crews, so we knew that we should not ask to work one of those districts. The Chief sat back in his big chair, sucking on the pipe that he always had, and asked us, "What makes you think you can all three work together? You know it is harder than hell to get three guys to work together." (Which, over the years, we found to be very true.) We replied, "Well, Chief, we came through the academy together and we've done a few things together and we all seem to get along."

He replied, "You mean you've done a lot of drinking together, don't you?" We all gulped, because that was very close to being the truth, as we had sat many nights in the police legion post, talking about working together. He then told us he would see what he could do.

We didn't hear anything from our Command or the Chief. However, when the sheet came down with the assignments two months later, all three of us were down for Unit 20, one of the Chief's favorite crews. Of course, we had to celebrate the new assignment at the post.

Our Crew

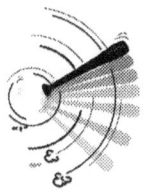

*T*his was a rather unique crew. Jeep was about 5'10" and weighed about 185 pounds. Lurch was 6'6" tall and weighed over 300 pounds. I was 6'1" and pushing about 275 pounds. Lurch and I never had much trouble when we worked together, but when either of us worked with Jeep, it seemed someone wanted to try and beat our ass more often than not.

Our district had three different housing projects in it and, around the homes, Lurch and I were known as "Mr. John" and "Mr. Mac". I was still in the National Guard at the time and came up with an idea. When John carried his old wooden nightstick in his hand, it looked like a toothpick as his hands were so big. I brought an ax handle home from the National Guard and we sanded it down and then stained and varnished it. If you wanted to see something bad, it was Lurch walking into the Cold Spot Cocktail Lounge at Avondale and Division with his new nightstick in his hand. It was quite impressive. Lurch never had to use the nightstick on anybody, but he sure would get their attention when he would smack the top of a table or bar with the ax handle. He was an awesome sight when he did this. There were so many people who become our friends in that district, as they were scared to death of "Gentle John".

Prior to joining the police department, Lurch had spent two years in a seminary, so the worst word that had ever came out of his mouth was "damnation". It only took a couple of months of working in the projects before he was spewing "fucking assholes".

Jeep had spent a couple of years as dispatcher for the Ohio Highway Patrol, prior to joining the Toledo Police Department. He had one of those photographic memories. They could read off a suspect or vehicle description at roll call and, two weeks later, he would spot the car or person fitting the description of the wanted person. From the time we left roll call on the second floor, till we got to the Sergeant's Desk on the first floor, John and I would forget any information.

I remember one time when we were working nights and Jeep spotted a new, red Pontiac Grand Prix with Ohio license plates on it. I was driving and Jeep told me to turn around and follow the Pontiac, as it was the one stolen from Roth Pontiac a couple of weeks ago. I told him he was full of shit. I turned around and started following the car and it went two blocks, where six black males bailed out and started running. We were close enough that we caught three of them and, sure as hell, it was the vehicle that was stolen from Roth Pontiac on Cherry street two weeks prior. Jeep's photographic memory came in handy many times over the years.

Just Like the Dukes of Hazzard

*I*t was a beautiful, clear, late spring day in 1967. Jeep was on a day off and I was working with Lurch. It was about 9:30 a.m. and we had just left the Safety Building, after completing a wagon call for another crew.

I was driving north on Michigan, approaching Cherry Street, when Unit 3 called for help and requested a "fast wagon" on Steele Street. As I mentioned earlier, whenever a crew called or dispatcher put out a fast wagon broadcast, every crew in the city that was "in-service" had to respond.

We informed the dispatcher of our location and he replied, "Step it up; you're the closest crew I have in-service." I turned from Michigan onto Cherry Street, headed east with our lights and sirens blasting away. The vehicle we were assigned was a 1965 Dodge Paddy Wagon. It looked like a regular panel truck painted black with the "Toledo Police" markings, a single revolving light on top, and a siren on the left front fender.

The Maumee River separates East Toledo from the rest of the City. At the time, there were only two bridges over the river. There was the Hi-Level bridge in South

Toledo, which was a suspension-type bridge and the Cherry Street Bridge, which was a "lift bridge" downtown. As we went through the light at Huron Street, heading for the Cherry Street Bridge, I could see ahead that traffic was stopped and then I noticed why. The bridge was on its way up so that a lake freighter could pass through on its way to the docks.

Unit #3 was screaming for help over the radio again, asking where the nearest crew was. The dispatcher told them that Unit 20 was approaching the Cherry Street Bridge and Unit #3 replied, "Tell them to step it up; we are really having a problem." I told Lurch, "Hold on; here we go." I drove to the left of center around all the stopped vehicles and was going at about 50 m.p.h. when I hit the ramp on its way up. I never looked down to see how far the two spans were apart when we jumped, but I know we hit with one helluva jolt and every bone in my body felt it when I landed on the other side. All Lurch did was yell, "You're fucking crazy," as we jumped the bridge.

We were the first crew there and able to assist Unit 3 in getting their suspect subdued and under arrest, without any of the Officers being seriously hurt. The two Officers on Unit #3 did receive minor treatment at the hospital after the incident.

As we headed back to the district, Lurch once again said, "I have never worked with someone as crazy you." He said he looked down as we were going over the bridge and all he could see was the water of the Maumee River.

Theft of a Mail Bag

On May 12, 1967, I was working the 3 to 11 shift with Jeep, and we had just picked up a prisoner on Franklin Avenue near the downtown area. Unit 10 had arrested the subject for public intoxication. I was driving and Jeep was in the back of the wagon with the prisoner. We were traveling south on Canton and had just passed through the intersection of Southard. The dispatcher was broadcasting the description of two black males, who had just stolen a bag of mail from a mail truck in front of the Family Court Center on Michigan, just off of Canton.

The dispatcher barely finished his broadcast, when I observed the two suspects running on the sidewalk, right towards us. Jeep had heard the dispatcher's transmission and I yelled, "Here they come, right at us!" I pulled the wagon to the curb and, as I jumped out of the front, Jeep was getting out of the back. I was able to grab the one suspect with the bag of mail, right at the rear of our wagon. Jeep took off, heading north on Canton, in pursuit of the other suspect. I notified the dispatcher that I had one of the mail thieves in custody and my partner was on foot pursuing the other suspect north on Canton towards Southard. I quickly handcuffed my suspect and put him in the rear of the wagon with our other prisoner.

I continued to watch Jeep in pursuit of the subject. I observed the suspect turn left between two buildings on Canton near Southard. Jeep was 15 to 20 feet behind the subject, and I could see him turn left between the two buildings. It seemed that Jeep was still in view, turning between the two buildings when I heard two gunshots. While I was watching this pursuit, I did not see that Jeep had his revolver out. I immediately notified the dispatcher that there now had been shots fired between my partner and the suspect. Of course, I thought the worst, as I had not seen Jeep remove his revolver. I assumed that when Jeep turned the corner, the suspect was waiting for him and fired at him.

The dispatcher immediately put out a broadcast for a "Fast wagon at Canton near Southard; shots fired; Officer from Unit #20 involved." Within what seemed only seconds, there were numerous crews arriving to assist us. Just as Unit #1 and Unit #10 pulled up to where I was with the two prisoners, Jeep came around the corner with the suspect in handcuffs.

I found out later that Jeep had pulled his gun out when he started the pursuit and, as he rounded the corner, he had fired two shots over the suspect's head. Back in those days, you were allowed to fire warning shots, but you still had to make out a report as to the circumstances under which you fired your weapon. This was done on what was called a Sergeant's Report. Just one copy was all that had to be made.

A month later, we both received a letter of Commendation from the U.S. Postal Service, the Toledo Police Department and the United States Federation of Police.

Downtown Pursuit of Suspect

*F*our days later, on May 16, 1967, I was working the 3 to 11 shift with Lurch. We were patrolling the downtown area around 4:45 p.m., with Lurch driving. We were on Monroe at Erie Street when the dispatcher put out a broadcast with a description of a black male wanted for theft, who was wearing a black leather jacket. He had taken numerous pairs of pants from the Lion Store at St. Clair and Adams Streets.

The suspect had been pursued outside of the store by off-duty Officer Foster Wiles, who was able to confront him at Superior and Adams. When the suspect turned to face Wiles, he had a small automatic in his hand and pulled the trigger twice. The suspect's gun misfired. The suspect threw the stolen pants at Wiles and took off running again. Wiles fired five shots at the suspect as he fled the scene. The suspect commandeered a car at Huron and Erie Street and told the driver to start driving. The driver of the vehicle stopped at the traffic light at Madison and Ontario and jumped out of the car. The suspect exited the vehicle and took off running south on Erie from Madison on the East Side of the street.

We had picked up Tim Szymankowski, another off-duty officer, who had been working at Lion Store and was also looking for the suspect. Tim had gotten on the back step of our wagon and was riding along with us. We were traveling north on Erie and had just crossed Jefferson, when we observed the suspect running towards Jefferson. He ran between two ladies who were also walking the same way and, as he passed them, he dropped the gun on the ground. The expressions on their faces were worth a hundred-thousand dollars.

I was in the passenger seat and we were moving along at about fifteen miles an hour in the curb lane. The suspect was looking over his shoulder and not paying attention to what was in front of him. As we got nearer to him, John hit the gas just as I jumped out of the wagon. I never missed a step running at the suspect and threw the most beautiful cross body block on him that I had ever managed. I wish my high school football coach could have seen that one. Anyway, as I hit him, the momentum carried us into the doorway of Roth Furs at 232 Erie Street. Of course, when we hit that door and window with the force we had, the burglar alarm siren went off, which caused even more chaotic activity.

Before I could get off the suspect, Officer Tim Szymankowski, who had followed right behind me, had his gun in the suspect's ear. All I could hear him say was, "Go ahead, motherfucker; move and see what happens." The suspect never said a word; I think he thought we were nuts. When we finally took him to the Detective Bureau, we found that he had been shot in the left arm. Apparently when he pulled the gun on Wiles and started running, Wiles had hit him with one of the rounds. We had to take him to Mercy Hospital for treatment.

He was charged with Grand Larceny, Carrying a Concealed Weapon, Assault with a Dangerous Weapon and Resisting Arrest.

Summer of 1967 – Civil Disturbances

$\mathcal{D}$uring the summer of 1967, the city was torn apart with civil disturbances. We were assigned to 12-hour shifts with no days off, and our shift was from 7:00 p.m. to 7:00 a.m. The morale of the entire department was the highest I had ever seen or ever saw again.

You were not allowed to take a call by yourself and every crew was there to back you up on each one. We were in the 600 block of Dorr one night and the dispatcher put out a call involving a man with a gun in the 900 block of Dorr, with shots fired. We were only three blocks away, but were the eighth crew on the scene.

That same night, a little later, we were dispatched to Bancroft and Franklin for a wagon call. When we arrived at the scene, there were three other crews there, who had a number of suspects lined up with their hands spread on the wall of a building and their legs spread apart. We were informed that they were all under arrest. We took them off the wall one by one, searched each one and then placed them in handcuffs and put them in the rear of the paddy wagon. We finally got them all in the back of the wagon and Jeep rode on the back step on the outside of the wagon, as there was no room for him to sit on the inside. As all of this was going on, we were getting bombarded with rocks and bottles, always with the sound of gunfire in the background.

I decided that I would not travel down any of the main streets to the jail, so I headed down one of the side streets. What a mistake that was. We were literally bombarded with everything the pedestrians could get their hands on and throw at us. Our windshield and passenger side door windows were cracked and we had numerous dents all over the wagon. Jeep was dodging projectiles all the way in. None of the projectiles ended up hitting us, so neither of us were injured.

The city fathers had placed a curfew in effect and all the bars had to be closed. We were dispatched along with five or six other crews, and one of our Lieutenants, to the G&H Bar on Dorr street, with the order to close it down. We all went in with our riot gear on.

There must have been 150 to 200 people in there, dancing away to the music. Our Lieutenant took his bullhorn and announced, "Your attention please. As of this minute, under City charter, this place is closed, as the City of Toledo is under curfew. You must leave immediately." He did this two or three more times and, you guessed it, not a single person paid attention to him.

Officer Bill Moseley, a black officer and a legend on the police department (more about him later in this book), went to the middle of the dance floor with a sawed-off shotgun, raised it into the air, and yelled, "This mutha fucking place is closed NOW!" He then pulled the trigger and discharged the shotgun into the ceiling. The place was emptied in less than two minutes. Even the bartender took off, leaving the cash register open. The Lieutenant just shook his head. We secured the building and left without a problem.

One other night during the riots, Jeep and I had just relieved the Officers at the barricades at Dorr and Junction, so they could get something to eat and drink. We were allowed to bring our own weapons in and carry them during the Civil Disturbances. I had brought my dad's shotgun to work with me and was carrying that in the wagon with us. It was almost the end of our tour for the day and this was the third or fourth day in a row that we had worked the 12-hour shift, leaving us exhausted.

We decided, while waiting there for the Officers to come back from their break, that we would get our gear together, so we would be ready to "hit off" when our shift was complete for the day. My dad's shotgun held six shells and the department's shotguns held four shells. I was standing on the driver's side of the wagon with the door open and Jeep was on the passenger side. We had switched positions during the night. Jeep had driven the first half of the shift and I was driving the second half.

We were gathering our equipment and I grabbed my dad's shotgun. Forgetting that we changed during the shift, I ejected four shells, thinking that was all there was, as the department's shotgun had been on my side during the night. After I ejected the fourth shell, I pulled the trigger. The shotgun was pointed towards the passenger side of the wagon when it went off. If I had been holding that shotgun about 12 inches higher, it probably would have cut Jeep in half. Instead, it went through part of the driver's seat and into our equipment box that fit perfectly between the two seats, forcing the side of the equipment box into the passenger seat.

After we both got our breath back, we were able to laugh about it. Actually, it was a very scary situation. When we were able to get the box out from between the seats, we were able to start laughing again. Everything in our box, including the crime reports, had a hole right through the middle, about three inches in diameter. Our nightsticks were wooden and all that was left was about three to four inches of the handle.

Of course when everyone heard the gunshot, ten or twelve crews responded immediately. A sergeant, who just happened to go by when the empty shell was ejected on to the hood of his car, started canceling crews, telling the dispatcher it was just a vehicle backfiring.

Stories About DaMoe

*I*n the mid 1960's, three black officers went to the Chief and requested to work together as a Unit on the 8 p.m. to 4 a.m. shift. This was the Chief's prize shift and he called it the high crime shift, as it had been determined that most felony crimes occurred during those hours. The chief thought it over for about a month and then put it into effect. The crews on this shift were designated by a number in the 580's, and each Unit covered anywhere from three to five regular districts. They were to handle only felony calls.

The all-black crew was to be known as Unit 600 and they were to cover the entire city. This was the first all-black crew to work together as a permanent crew. The Officers were Bill Moseley, Marcus McCardy and Woodruff Crady. They were able to handle problems in the inner city in much different ways than a mixed crew or an all-white crew could. The people living in the projects and inner city either respected this crew or were scared to death of them. When they informed the public of something, they knew that they had better adhere to what they were told.

One instance I remember very well occurred when we were working the 11 p.m. to 7 a.m. shift. There had been a number of calls, almost every night, involving the Sandnoy Night Club on Hawley near Nebraska. The complaints included disturbances, loud noise, assaults, and hundreds of persons congregating on the sidewalks and in the streets around closing time.

Unit 600 had decided that they were going to clean up the area by making their presence known. One particular night, they had been sent to the Sandnoy Night Club on two different occasions before 11:00 p.m., concerning disturbances and loud noises. Around 1:00 a.m., we were dispatched there, along with Unit 600, on a complaint of numerous persons loitering and causing disturbances in front of the building. We arrived at the scene at the same time as Unit 600 and noted that there were about one hundred and fifty people milling around on the sidewalks and in the street.

We all exited the police vehicles and Bill, in his booming voice, making sure he got everyone's attention said, "If I have to come back here another time tonight, any muthafucker standing on this sidewalk or in the street is going to get hurt and hurt bad and then their sorry ass is going to jail. Do you all understand what DaMoe has just told you?" There were no answers, just mumblings and noddings of heads. Bill then said to them, "Good, now get the fuck out of here." The crowd slowly dispersed, some wandering away, others going back into the club.

Bill suggested to us that we should stay in the area, but not be seen, as he said, "I'm going to have to show them that DaMoe means what he says." Bill suggested that we park the wagon down the street in the alley on the eastern side of the street, and he and his partner would be on the other side. We decided that if Bill was going to make a move towards the club, he would signal us by blinking his lights and we would follow him out of the alley to the scene.

It was about fifteen minutes later when I observed Bill blink his lights and start out of the alley heading towards the corner of Hawley and Nebraska, squealing tires as he went. We were right behind them and could see there were a number of persons congregating on the sidewalks and streets in front of the Sandnoy Nite Club.

All of a sudden, Unit 600 goes up over the curb, down the sidewalk, right towards the large group of people, slowing a little as he proceeded. I never saw anything like it, there were bodies flying everywhere, trying to dive out of the way of the police unit. Unit 600 came to a full stop in front of the Sandnoy and all I could hear was some of these people yelling, "That crazy muthafucker!" We just started grabbing bodies and placing them in the back of the wagon.

Once again, Bill had to make his speech to make sure everyone knew that the "Moe" meant business. We never had a problem again for the rest of that month at this location, and very few after that. Apparently, they finally realized that DaMoe meant what he said.

One other story about DaMoe, I remember vividly, as I was again involved. We were working the 11 to 7 shift and it was a nice, clear, rather warm night in June. We were dispatched, along with Unit 600, to a burglary in progress call at the State Liquor store at the Swayne Field Shopping Center at Monroe and Detroit. The dispatcher informed us that entry had been made in the rear of the store. Unit 600 stated that they would come in from the east end of the shopping center.

We then responded that we would enter from the other end. As we entered at the rear of the shopping center, we observed a black male exiting the rear of the liquor store with something in his hands. The suspect saw us, dropped what he had in his hands and started running the other way, just as Unit 600 came in from the other direction. He looked like a scared "rat".

Along the back of the property behind the shopping

center was a nine-foot chain-length fence that ran along the entire length of the property, about thirty feet from the rear of the buildings. The suspect stopped in his tracks when he saw that a police crew was approaching him from both directions. The suspect first looked in our direction then turned in the direction of Unit 600. He then starting fleeing towards the chain-length fence at full speed.

As he got to the fence, he immediately started scaling the fence, as we were now approaching him. He was at the top of the fence when Bill "DaMoe" Moseley ran his police car into the bottom of the fence. Upon impact, like a slingshot, the suspect first went one way and then the other, as the fence whipped back. The suspect lost his grip and flew to the ground right in front of our police vehicles. We were out of our vehicles and had the suspect handcuffed before he could stagger to his feet. He looked at DaMoe and said, "You are fucking crazy, man."

We found that he had been carrying the cash drawer and two bottles of whiskey when we first observed him exiting the liquor store. The suspect had to be taken to the hospital for treatment from his fall, with bruises and lacerations to his arms, legs and face.

Don't Mess With Lurch

I was working a day shift with Lurch on the 3 to 11 shift, when we received a call to assist Sergeant Dick Gladieux with a Driving Under Arrest. We arrived at the scene and could see that the suspect was practically without the use of his legs. He had almost driven his vehicle head-on into the Sergeant's police car. We had a little scuffle with the suspect at the scene, but nothing out of the ordinary. Lurch rode in the back of the wagon with the suspect. His name, which I will never forget, was Dantel Hope.

I was driving the paddy wagon and could hear the conversation in the back through the window between the front and back of the wagon. I heard Dantel mutter in a slurred voice, "White man, I'm going to beat your ass." The next thing I saw in the rear view mirror was Dantel leaping out of his seat, as his fist connected with Lurch's jaw. That would be the last time that Dantel struck Lurch.

I stopped the wagon, got out, and proceeded to the back of the wagon to see if Lurch needed any assistance. When I opened the rear door, Lurch was on top of the suspect and Dantel was screaming that he had had enough. Lurch had one welt on the side of his jaw, but Dantel looked a lot worse off.

We got to the fifth floor of the Safety Building where the Men's Jail was located and placed Dantel in the drunkometer room. We then waited for the Sergeant to give the Breathalyzer. Dantel was sitting in the chair and I had him stand up so I could remove the handcuffs, as it seemed he had settled down. Dantel looked up at Lurch and said, "White man, I gonna try your ass one more time." Dantel started to get up and, as he rushed for Lurch, Lurch put out his big hand and placed it on the back of Dantel's head, pushing him right past him into a steel door. Dantel went down and out for the count. We had to take him to the hospital to get patched up.

Dantel decided that he had better calm down by the time we took him back to the jail for his drunkometer test. He was sitting across the table from Sergeant John Dolding (a true Irishman), who was going to administer the test. Sergeant Dolding asked Dantel, "How many beers have you had to drink, Mr. Hope?" He answered, "Two Beers, sir." Sergeant Dolding responded in his booming Irish voice, "Two beers, my ass… two barrels maybe!" Dantel refused to take the test at that time, so he was booked and placed in his cell. He must have pleaded guilty in court, as we never had to testify against him.

The Accident

On a warm Sunday night, on August 27, 1967, around 8:30 p.m., I was working with Jeep on our usual wagon district, Unit 20. We had just picked up a prisoner (intoxicated) from Canton and Woodruff for Unit #10. I was driving and Jeep was in the back compartment with the prisoner.

We had just been issued one of the new Ford paddy wagons. It was a lot larger than the one we had been driving in the past. They were large and bulky and looked like an ice cream truck.

Our vehicle had only been in service a few days and had a total of 1,493 miles on it. We were southbound on Michigan, just entering the intersection at Adams, traveling around 25 m.p.h. with the traffic light green, when an eastbound vehicle on Adams Street struck us on the passenger side of the wagon. The impact drove us to the left, up over the curb, shearing off a traffic signal. I felt the two crashes and saw that I was headed straight for a steel light pole. I attempted to swerve to avoid the pole, but I hit the pole head on. I could not have hit it more direct center than I did.

When I saw the collision with the steel pole coming, I threw my left arm up in front of my face and, upon impact, my left forearm and wrist went through the windshield. My right knee went into the dashboard and my left leg was up under the dash. I was able to look around through the window behind me into the rear of the wagon and could see Jeep and the prisoner in a heap. I could see blood on Jeep's head and he appeared to be unconscious.

I was able to stretch my right arm out to reach the microphone cord and managed to pull the cord to the end and grab hold of the microphone. I keyed the mike and informed the dispatcher: "We were involved in a serious-injury accident at Michigan and Adams. Please send help." Immediately, I heard nothing but sirens and crew after crew stating over the airwaves that they were responding.

I learned later that, around this time, my parents and brother and his girlfriend were at my house. Mom had just tried to tune the police radio in and was having a tough time finding the police broadcasts. Back then, the police radios in the homes had dials and you had to keep tuning them in. The first thing my mother heard on the police band was my call for help. My brother and his girlfriend took off in his car and headed to the scene.

The responding Officers and firemen were able to get the injured persons from the other car, along with Jeep and the prisoner, into ambulances and on their way to the hospital. I was still trapped in the cab of the truck, and the rescue Squad and Officers were having one helluva time trying to get me out. I remember lying there in the cab with my left arm bleeding and no feeling in my legs and unable to move. All at once, I heard a female voice saying, "Let me through; that's my brother-in-law." That really threw me for a loop, as all the other injured persons had been removed and I had no sister-in-law at the time. It was my brother's girlfriend trying to get through the police line.

The rescue squad back in those days did not have any of the equipment that they have nowadays, like the "jaws of life". They were having a problem getting the driver's door open, as it buckled upon impact with the steel pole. The passenger door was up against the old Masonic Building that was on the southeast corner of Michigan and Adams. A number of the officers and firemen were trying to loosen the door by using crowbars, pry bars, and whatever else they could get their hands on, but to no avail.

Finally Dave Perkins, a fairly big guy, who was working the Accident Investigation Unit, said, "Let me give it a try. I'll get him out; that's my buddy." (Dave and I had walked the East Toledo foot patrols quite a bit.) Dave got his hands in between the door and the jamb and, with numerous grunts and groans, almost pulled the damn door off the hinges. When he was finished and let go, the door was hanging by one hinge.

I could hear a Command Officer on the radio telling the dispatcher to start putting some of the crews back in service. The dispatcher responded and said, "I am leaving all the crews out of service, Lieutenant, until all the injured officers are on their way to the Hospital. They are my responsibility, Lieutenant." Not another word was said.

The rescue squad and officers were then able to slide me down a little and relieve the pressure on the left leg that was up under the dash, but they were still not able to get my right knee removed from the dash. Part of the dashboard had to be removed, and only then were they able to lift me out onto the stretcher. The ambulance then took off and took me to Mercy Hospital. I was wheeled into the emergency room and placed in one of the cubicles.

On the other side of the hallway they put Jeep in a cubicle right next to an elderly man. I was conscious, but unable to move my legs, no matter how hard I tried.

Sergeant Dick Parton, who was my district Sergeant, was asking questions about the accident, along with Dan Portkins, the investigator. They kept saying to me, "The light was green, wasn't it, O.J?" I kept saying, "Yeah, I think it was green." Once again, they said, "The light was green, wasn't it, O.J?" And then, I caught on that I was not supposed to say I thought it was green; I was supposed to say it definitely was green.

The emergency room was full of police officers by now, along with Jeep's and my family. I heard a few of the Officers say that Jeep was in bad shape and had not regained consciousness, as of yet. A priest was seen going into Jeep's room. So of course, about five or six of the officers came into my cubicle to inform me that the priest was performing the last rites on Jeep. Boy did I feel like shit then. I thought my partner and friend was dead. We found out a few minutes later that the priest was there to perform the last rites on the old man, who was in the cubicle next to Jeep, as he had died. I did feel a little better after that.

Jeep was sent to the Intensive Care Unit, and I was admitted to a room with three other patients. There was not a whole lot of privacy in these rooms. I had a number of tests during the next two to three days, while they tried to find out why I had no feeling in my legs. On the fourth day, Jeep was released from intensive care. The hospital then made a mistake. One of the patients in my room had been discharged, so they put Jeep in the same room with me. There were policemen in our room visiting us almost twenty-four hours a day.

The feeling came back into my legs on the sixth day in the hospital. Jeep ended up with a fractured skull, along with other injuries. I ended up with a broken wrist and two messed-up knees. The right knee needed two surgeries on it over the years. I was unable to go back to work until February of 1968. During this time, Jeep and I found it very boring sitting home doing nothing. Our doctors told us we should get out and do things and move around a little.

Jeep and I went to see the Chief, because department regulations at the time stated that, if you were off sick or injured, you were to be at your place of residence. We told the Chief what the doctors had said. We told him we would like to get out of our houses at night once in a while and would like to get his permission to do so. The Chief replied to us, "You want to go to the Police Post and drink, don't you!" Of course, we said we didn't. He said it was okay with him, as long as we stayed away from the Post. Well, that we did. We did our drinking at the Molehouse on South Erie Street, instead.

Jeep went back to work around November on light duty in the Record Bureau. My doctor would not let me go back to work yet, even on light duty. My family doctor sent me to see an orthopedic specialist, as my right knee was not responding to any type of treatment. The orthopedic doctor tried everything from physical therapy to draining the water on my knee, but to no avail.

Finally, surgery was scheduled for January 4th. One problem, though. I went out with Jeep and a few other friends and officers the night before and got smashed. I was so bad that, when they took my blood the next day, they informed me the alcohol content in my blood was too high and the surgery had to be postponed for another day. The surgery went well, but the knee was a lot worse than the doctor expected. A plastic kneecap had to be put in and a lot of cartilage had to be removed. I developed phlebitis in the right leg and they watched that very closely every day.

I was finally able to go back to work on light-duty in February on midnights in the Record Bureau, along with Jeep. It was a long time before I was able to work the street again.

Moving West ~ Back to Work

I worked light duty from February 1968 until the summer of 1968, when my doctor finally released me for full street duty. I was again working with Jeep and we were assigned to Unit 18, which covered a lot of deep West Toledo, all the way to the state line.

After working the inner city, it was very hard to get accustomed to working in an area where people actually waved at the police, rather than threw things at them. While we were patrolling the side streets, people would actually want us to stop, so they could talk to a police officer. Jeep and I worked together, along with Marvin Fleckner, who later became Chief; Tom Cartbell, who later attained the rank of Lieutenant; and Fred Carpeto.

During the time that Jeep, Marvin, and I worked together, we earned quite a reputation in West Toledo. We averaged 150 movers (traffic citations) a month, when we were on either the 3 to 11 or 11 to 7 shift. We never really bothered too much with the people on the day shift, but the troublemakers knew that when we were on either of the night shifts, they had better not misbehave. We had put together a loose-leaf notebook that we carried in our vehicle and it had every "chicken shit" offense in it. We called this book of information, our "Unit 18 Punkie Book." We looked all through the Toledo Municipal Traffic Code and the State Code book for every unknown offense we could find. We even had the manufacturer's book on height requirements for bumpers of cars. Needless to say, one of our tools in our equipment box was a tape measure. We used a code under "riding where not designed" a lot. This is when the girls used to sit on the console next to the guy while he was driving. Not only could she be cited, but the operator could also be cited for allowing that person to sit there.

The White Hut at Sylvania & Secor was a hangout for teens back then and we used to patrol that area quite frequently. We got to know the car hops very well. One night, one of the girls had a red welt on the side of her face. When we asked her what happened, she told us that a guy she used to date had slapped her alongside the head that night. We asked her if she wanted a report made, so she could prosecute if she wanted to. She did not want to prosecute, but we told her we would take the report just in case anything else might happen between them. We told her we would make sure he was taken care of.

He was not very hard to spot. He drove a 1967 Plymouth Barracuda, candy-apple red in color. It was called the "Bad Apple Cuda." Kids in those days used to have names for their cars and it would usually be painted on the rear fenders of the vehicle. We spread the word to the other crews in the area about this car and what the driver had done to one of the car hops at the drive-in restaurant.

Within a few weeks, this particular vehicle was cited for committing nine different traffic violations. For quite a while after that, none of us saw the car in the area. But, the next thing we knew, the car was in the lot at Grogan Used Car lot on Jackman Road, and it was for sale.

First Time Playing Santa

$\mathcal{T}$he Police Post was sponsored by the American Legion and was located in the 2200 block of Ashland Avenue. It was a place where officers could go after work and have a drink. Usually, there was no one in there but police officers and close friends or families of police officers. When you got off work and wanted to have a drink, you just put your gun and police shirt in the trunk of your car and went and had a drink, or two, at the Police Post.

At the time, the place was very active and going strong. There were always a good number of officers present having a drink or playing cards. Lt. Dan "Brute" Schiffler and Lt. Carl Wilson were managing the facility. If you volunteered and bartended two four-hour shifts during a month, Brute and Carl would throw a party at the end of the month for all those who had volunteered.

These parties were usually held at either Brute's or Carl's house. Brute had one of those good ol' Catholic families. I think he had eight or nine children. They lived in one of those big houses in the 2500 block of Scottwood. The houses had three or four floors, some with elevators installed.

The American Legion's Christmas party for the kids was to be held at the Police Post. Because I had the build for it, Brute suggested that I play Santa Claus for the kid's party. I finally told him I would do it, but it would cost him a meal and some drinks for the Jolly Old Elf. It was held on a Saturday afternoon and I got there early and took the outfit and accessories upstairs. Everything at the Post took place on the first floor, so I knew I would have privacy upstairs.

To pass the time, I had a few beers, while waiting to make my appearance. As time passed, I could hear a lot of commotion downstairs. I walked partway down the stairs to see what was going on. All I could see were a bunch of screaming kids. There must have been over a hundred of them. I told Brute to bring me a couple more beers, which he did. A while later, word was sent up to me that they would be ready in fifteen minutes for the arrival of Santa Claus. I put the outfit on, along with the makeup, eyebrows, beard and all, and was ready to go. By now I was feeling pretty relaxed – I mean I was feeling real good.

This was my first time playing Santa and I was a little worried that I would not do a good job. I had the five or six beers in me by then and I felt very much at ease. I went down the steps and yelled loudly, "Merry

Christmas Everyone!" The kids screamed… they loved me. (Can't say as I blame them.) I proceeded over to the crowd and sat down in the chair they had prepared for Santa to sit in.

The parents lined up with their darling children and started bringing the kids to me. It went very well, with the only problem being that one of Jack Dolding's kids, after being on my lap, went back to him and said, "Daddy, Santa Claus's breath smells just like yours!"

This was the first of many times I would play Santa for organizations and individuals, and it is something I still do to this day.

Brute asked me to come to his house one night to play Santa for his whole family and I agreed to do it. Needless to say, Brute's family was huge. It not only was his immediate family, but his brothers, sisters, and their kids. I remember Brute telling me that he had a brother who was a priest.

When I got to the house, there were a crowd of people and kids there. The living room was humongous. The house was very warm and I was hotter than hell and sweating profusely in the outfit and beard.

After I distributed the gifts and said goodbye to the kids, I went out into the hallway and Brute asked how I was doing. There were two or three people standing around him and I said, "Damn, I'm hot, where's the goddamn beer? I need a drink."

Everyone laughed as Brute introduced me to his brother, the Priest. I felt like two cents. However, the priest was laughing too, so I guess I won't be going to hell over that one.

Automobile Club Adventures

*J*eep and I started projecting (working off-duty jobs) at the Automobile Club on Ashland Avenue, just two doors from the post, teaching driver's training. We were earning $4.00 an hour at the Auto Club, which was not bad back then. We averaged between 20 and 25 hours a week during our off-duty hours. I found that girls were much easier to teach to drive than guys were. The guys thought they knew it all – you know, like using one finger to turn the steering wheel. The most difficult students to teach were nuns and foreign doctors. Damn, they would put a death grip on that steering wheel that you couldn't pry loose. I was fortunate enough to meet my lovely wife while I was employed at the Auto Club.

One night I had a young black male for his first driving lesson. He had just completed his classroom instructions and was ready for the road. One of the first questions you would ask a new student was if he or she had any prior driving experience. Almost all of them had at least been behind the wheel once before they took the course. When I inquired of this student he replied, "No sir." I wondered just who he was trying to bullshit. Every kid in those days had driven a little before they started their lesson. I soon found that this kid was NOT kidding.

We started out of the parking lot onto Ashland Avenue and I had him make a right turn. As he made the turn, he held onto the wheel and did not let it come back. We ended up over the curb and on the sidewalk. He was as nervous as hell. I calmed him down a little and, when we got back on the road, I had him go east on Ashland. As we approached Bancroft, I told him to make another right turn. Once again, he made the turn with ease, but held onto the wheel again. Thank God for the brake on my side of the vehicle. Back on the sidewalk we went, once again. I got him back on the street and told him we would make a right turn on Collingwood. This time, he made the turn and all he did was hit the curb. I told him to proceed North on Collingwood and we would make another right turn into the Auto Club parking lot. I had made up my mind that I would have to keep this student off the streets for a while.

As we approached the back entrance driveway, I had him make a right turn. When we got to the back drive of the Auto Club, I had him make the right turn again. He made it, but I don't know how. I had him stop the vehicle for a few minutes after we entered the driveway and tried to have him relax a little and get himself together. After a while, I thought he had settled down enough, so I had him proceed to make only right turns around the Auto Club building. For thirty minutes, all we did was make right turns around the building. I figured having him in the parking lot was the safest place, as there were not any cars in the vicinity of the building and no curbs to bounce off or go over.

We had about fifteen minutes to go and had just about made a complete turn at the back corner of the building. There was one car in the entire parking lot at the rear of the building. I didn't know where it came from, as it was not there the last time we came around the building. Later that day, I was informed that it was an employee who had just arrived at work.

I do not know what happened to my student, but as he came out of the last turn, he panicked, had his foot floored to the gas pedal and a death grip on the steering wheel. He was headed right for that only car in the parking lot. I stood on the brake on my side of the car, attempting to stop the car, as I grabbed the steering wheel trying to turn it. But he had one of those "death grips" on the steering wheel. He hit that car squarely in the right front, and the force of the impact lifted the parked car off the ground.

He could not have hit that car more squarely. No one was injured even with the extensive damage to both vehicles, and I have to admit that was the only accident I had there, until I quit in 1972. That was the last time I had him for a lesson, and I do not know how he finished up.

The Drag Racers

*J*eep and I were working together one night, when the expressway around Toledo was under construction. A section of it was open between Talmadge and Secor Roads, just about a mile in length. We received a lot of complaints that this section of the expressway was being used for drag racing. We found that we were able to enter from Talmadge Road, back up and park under the Talmadge Road overpass and sit there undetected. Many times we would sit there and catch up on reports when there was no activity. We had informed the dispatchers on our shift of our "hideout" and they gave it the name of "The Bat Cave".

Sitting in the "Bat Cave," we could observe traffic westbound and eastbound on that section of the express-way and remain undetected. We would sit there and observe vehicles traveling slow westbound, looking for police vehicles. They would then exit and cross over the expressway on Talmadge Road and enter eastbound. When they got to the bottom of the ramp, and were assured that no police vehicles were around, they would take off eastbound, racing each other.

Whenever we observed this activity, we would exit the "Bat Cave" with lights flashing and siren screaming and pull the suspects over. We became so efficient at timing our thrust out of the "Bat Cave" that we would usually stop them before they traveled more than a third of a mile.

One night, as we removed one of the drivers from his car, we recognized that it was one of our students who had just finished driver's training with us, about two weeks prior. He was rather embarrassed and, after he received a good ass chewing from Jeep and I, we had the vehicle towed and took the subject home.

We explained to the parents that we had just caught him drag racing on the expressway and that we had been his driving instructors just two weeks before then. I am sure the punishment he received at home was much more severe than the one he received when he went to court.

One other instance I remember about our "Bat Cave" experiences is the night we chased two cars and one car stopped, but the other decided he was going to run from us. The problem was this kid was not a Rhodes Scholar, as he did not realize that the expressway ended on the overpass at Secor Road. He hit the end of the pavement of the overpass at a speed in excess of 60 m.p.h., went airborne and landed in a sea of mud. The car sunk in the mud up to its wheel wells. We did not have to go in after him, as he knew he had been had and dragged himself out to us.

This is another one that we took home and left it to the father to take care of the punishment, in addition to the sentencing from the courts. The bill for removing the vehicle from the mud had to be very expensive, as it took two tow trucks over two hours to remove it.

Little Off District

*W*hile working Unit 18, my partners and I were always being harassed by our command, because they thought we were screwing around too much and having too much fun. I guess you were not supposed to enjoy yourself on the job. Yet, we always had more than enough traffic citations and arrests each month.

There was not a quota that we had to meet, as most citizens seemed to think, but there was an old saying that went: "A mover a day, keeps the Sergeant away." That was something every police officer never had to worry about, as so many traffic violations occurred every day, right in plain view, and there was no reason you couldn't issue one citation each day. That one citation just might have saved a person's life.

The Sergeants on our shift were always trying to catch us off district or involved in some other department violation. One night, we were working 11 to 7 and it was about 2:30 in the morning. It had been a very slow night up to this point. I had a slight cold and decided I would slip home to get some cold medicine. I was still living with my parents in West Toledo, just about six blocks from our district. In order to remain undetected, we drove on all the side streets to my house. I went in, got the cold medicine, which took all of 45 seconds, came out and we started heading back to district.

As we approached Upton and Berdan, a car turned off Upton onto Berdan, right in front of us, squealing its tires and accelerating at a high rate of speed. Jeep was driving and we looked at each other and said, "Let's stop him, but don't put it on the air because of our location." So we turned on our lights and siren and tried to pull him over. Just as we were able to get behind the suspect vehicle, he made a left turn onto one of the side streets and started running from us.

We didn't dare put the chase on the air, because we were so far off district, and we knew we would get our asses chewed. The chase went on for about ten minutes, up and down the side streets, slowly getting closer to our district boundary.

Finally, the suspect vehicle was within a few blocks of our district and, thank God, because he struck two parked cars near Beaufort and Douglas. We decided at this point to put the information regarding the suspect vehicle out over the air to the other crews. Within minutes there were about four other crews involved in the chase. It finally ended up in front of the University of Toledo on Bancroft. The suspect exited the vehicle and, after a short chase, was apprehended by an officer working the Accident Investigation Unit that night. The suspect came up fighting after being apprehended by the officer and a slight tussle occurred between the suspect and a few officers trying to subdue the suspect. It turned out that the suspect's vehicle was a stolen car from a dealership in the area.

While we were involved in the tussle and putting some handcuffs on the subject, we noticed that Safety Director, Clinton Quarton, was at the scene. Other crews had many times informed us that he would show up at the scene of an investigation, especially during the night-time shifts.

This night, Director Quarton was telling all of us what a fine job we had done, as no one had been hurt and the suspect was in custody. At the same time, our district Sergeant was chewing us out for not having our coats buttoned or hats on.

The Safety Director informed the Sergeant to write the crews up for a job well done. I guess the "attaboy" outweighed the ass chewing. Quarton was one of the most active Safety Directors during the time I was on the police department.

West Toledo Warfare

*W*hile working west Toledo, there were many, many nights that were very slow and many nights when our Unit would go without getting dispatched to a call. West Toledo was a very low-crime area and not the most populated area of the City at the time. The City was still growing and west was the only way it could grow. To pass the time on some nights, crews used to pull practical jokes on each other.

We used to hit off by telephone at the end of our tour at Douglas and Sylvania at the call box. These call boxes were made of cast iron so they were very durable. One morning after working the 11 to 7 shift, we pulled up to the corner of Sylvania and Douglas, the location where we were to "hit off." I exited the police car and opened the call box door. As I did, an egg fell out of the call box, landed on my shoe, and broke. In the box was a handwritten note that read, "Ha Ha, the yokes on you," and it was signed, "The Phantom". We were certain that Unit 22 was the culprit that played the practical joke. We vowed to get even.

We knew that Unit 22 would stop a few times a week at a house on the edge of their district that adjoins ours. They would stop there, as it was a relative of one of the officers working the crew. He would fix them breakfast in the early morning and they would listen to the police monitor that the relative had in his house. We still did not have portable radios at the time on the department, so the only communication you had with the dispatcher was with the radios in the police cars. This relative had a police radio monitor that was very popular back then, as citizens would listen to police calls.

Whenever Unit 22 stopped at this house, they would pull the car into the drive and park at the back of the house. Both officers would go in and eat breakfast with the relative and listen to the police monitor and, if they received a call from the dispatcher, they could go to the car and answer the call.

Jeep and I were working together one night when Unit 22 had stopped at this house for breakfast. We had driven by and accidentally spotted their police car in the driveway.

We came to the conclusion it was time to get even for the egg on the shoe. I parked our car about two houses away and Jeep walked back to the location where the vehicle was parked in the driveway. He quietly walked up the drive, opened the car door and found the keys were in the vehicle. He turned the key in the ignition to loosen the steering wheel and then nudged the vehicle a little so that it rolled down the drive into the street. Once the vehicle was in the street, I assisted Jeep in pushing the vehicle about three houses down the street. We were able to get back in our car just about the time our District Sergeant was polling his crews for mail.

Near the end of each shift, the District Sergeant would contact his crews for what was called "mail". These were the reports, citations, and other paperwork that the crew had taken during their tour of duty. The Sergeant then would check the reports, citations and other paperwork to make sure they were filled out correctly.

We pulled our police car across the street and down a few houses and parked under a tree where we could not be seen, yet had full view of the house. When the Sergeant polled us for mail, we answered that we had none. Unit 22 was next and, when the Sergeant polled them, we observed one officer exit the rear door of the house and stop in the middle of the drive, looking around for the car.

We heard him yell, "Bob, the damn car is gone; someone must have stolen it." The next thing we see is both officers running down the drive to the street looking both ways and finally spotting their car three houses down from their location.

Meanwhile, the Sergeant has called them a second time, as they had not answered yet. They reached the car, just as the Sergeant called for the third time. The Sergeant asked them, "Have you been copying my transmission? This is the third time I've tried to call you." The crew answered, "We've tried to answer Sergeant, but there must have been something wrong with the microphone and we do not have any mail." Unit 22 informed us, at the end of our tour, that they would get even someday.

On another long quiet night, Jeep and I decided that we would pull another practical joke on Unit 22 and sabotage their hit off box. Their hit off point was supposed to be at Bancroft and Parkside, but they would always sneak down and hit off at Bancroft and Auburn, which was closer to Downtown by about a mile and a half.

During the night, we had obtained a large paper cup from one of the drive-in restaurants on our district. On our way to Bancroft and Auburn, in the early morning hours, we stopped by the firehouse and filled the cup with water.

We continued on to the call box location. We opened the call box, placed the large cup of water in the call box, and tied a string to the cup and the other end of the string to the call box door. Then we took some fingerprint ink that we carried in our equipment box and smeared it on the earpiece and the inside handle of the phone. When Unit 22 opened the call box door, we knew they would pull on it quickly, because of the weight of the door and the fact that it usually stuck a little, and the water would come out and land on them or their feet.

After completing our dastardly deed, we headed back towards our district to await the hit off time.

Meanwhile, the day shift Sergeant, Lee Deal who had just been promoted not more than a couple of weeks before then, was on the street and asked to meet Unit 12, Unit 22, and Unit 122 at Monroe & Upton. There was a labor strike at Doehler Jarvis on Smead Avenue, and they wanted the crews to be prepared for any trouble that morning. The dispatcher asked Sergeant Deal to call their office by phone, in the event that they had further information for him to pass on to the crews. The Sergeant said he would inform him from the call box at Monroe and Auburn.

The next radio conversation we heard was Sergeant Deal asking the dispatcher if he was getting a light on the box at Monroe and Auburn. The dispatcher answered no, and Deal then told him he would call from Bancroft and Auburn, and have those crews meet him there. I figured we were in real trouble then. The next thing we knew, every west end crew is getting called into the day shift's Captain's Office, as they reported off duty.

Each crew was called in and questioned about the sabotaging of the call box at Bancroft and Auburn, except us. To this day, I still cannot figure why we were not questioned about it.

Unit 22 figured out who it was, but they never let on to anyone about their suspicions. They told us that they were there when the Sergeant unlocked the door and started opening the door of the call box. They observed him stop, after he had just opened the door part way. He reached in the callbox, untied the string, and with a smile on his face, just shook his head as he removed the cup of water. The Sergeant then removed the phone handle from the call box and called the dispatcher.

When he finished the call, one of the officers standing there told him that he had something black on his right ear. The Sergeant instinctively reached up with his right hand and rubbed his right ear. The fingerprint ink was all over his ear, the side of his face and, by then, his right hand.

About a year later, Lee Deal saw me in the hallway of the Safety Building, and he mentioned to me about being a victim of the West Toledo warfare. He said he had promised one of the Officers from Unit 22 that he would never mention it to me that he knew that I did it, as he had participated in West Toledo Warfare in his earlier days.

He said he was so proud of himself when he opened the call box and saw the string. He reached inside and untied the string and lifted the cup out and sat it on the ground. He picked up the phone and called the dispatcher. When he hung the phone up someone asked, "What in the hell is that on your ear?" He took his hand and rubbed his ear and now the fingerprint ink was all over the side of his head and his hand. If you ever had any experience with that stuff, you know it just keeps spreading. Well, before he knew it, it was all over his brand new white Sergeant's shirt.

Of course, no one there at Bancroft and Auburn knew anything about it. I'm glad it was some time later that Lee found out who did it and was able to laugh about it.

Lee was promoted to Lieutenant and then Captain before he retired as one of the most respected Captains on the police department.

It seems like all of my stories about Unit 18 have to do with the "West Toledo Warfare" stories. It was Halloween night one year, and I was working with Jeep again. One of our first calls that night was to see a complainant about an item thrown from an overpass in West Toledo. We arrived at the complainant's house and he was furious at first, but then laughed about the incident that had occurred earlier. He had been outbound on Monroe and had just passed under the underpass near Swayne Field when someone threw a life-size dummy out in front of his car. He had to hit the brakes and swerve, almost causing an accident to avoid hitting this "person". He got out of car and picked it up, put it in his trunk and took it home.

I must say this "Dummy" really looked good. It had a full head mask, rubber hands and feet and if you stood it up it looked like it was about 5'10" tall and weighed about 160 pounds. We told the gentleman that we would take the report and make sure someone kept an eye on the overpass. He asked if we were going to take the "dummy" with us, as he didn't want it around his house. I said, "Sure, we'll take care of it for you." Right away, our evil minds were at work.

Like I said earlier, the guys working Unit 22 were always messing with us. At this time, one of the Officers on the crew was running a landscape business that his dad had left him when he passed away.

The office of the landscape business was located in what used to be a large house trailer, and it was at Bancroft and Torrey Hill. The trailer had one big patio-type sliding glass door on the front of the trailer and another one on the backside. When it quieted down on district around 3:30 a.m., Jeep and I drove over to the trailer.

We took the "dummy" out of the trunk of our car and wrapped a rope around his shoulders and then hung it so it actually looked like it was on the inside of the trailer in the darkness. We then called the dispatcher by phone and told them to give Unit 22 a call about a man "hanging" around near the trailer at Torrey Hill and Bancroft.

We headed back to district and listened to our police radio to see what would transpire, if anything. A few minutes later, Unit 22 came on the air and said in a hurried voice, "Put us out here; we have someone inside, and send us some help."

Immediately after, Unit 17, the paddy wagon on the adjoining district, requested to be put out in the rear of that location. The next thing we heard was one of the two crews saying something into the microphone, and you could hear shots being fired. I just about died thinking about what the hell was going on.

Well, it turned out that Unit 17 had observed the suspect in the window from the rear at an angle from the Freeman Street side of the trailer and thought the suspect had a gun. They started firing at the trailer. Unit 22 heard the shots being fired and thought the guy inside was firing at them. Both crews were never shooting at each other, but they sure shot the shit out of that trailer.

Unit 22 came on the air and said, "You can cancel any command coming here, as we have everything under control." A few minutes later, the dispatcher asked Unit 22 if everything was all right. Unit 22 said, "Yes, we have everything under control. We got the one dummy here at the scene, but the Big Dummy (meaning me) got away and we'll get him later. Ho hum, just another chapter in the West Toledo Warfare.

Flying Donuts

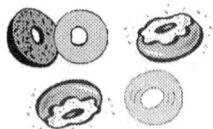

One other night, we got chewed out, but good, by our District Sergeant, concerning having two crews in the same restaurant at the same time. It was about 4:30 in the morning and we saw that Unit 17, a paddy wagon, was sitting in the parking lot at the White Hut at Secor and Monroe. We circled the block and came through slowly cruising the lot. As we approached their wagon, they said, "Come on and let's have a coffee."

I replied, "No thanks, the sergeant is probably watching for us to do something like that." As I pulled past the rear of the wagon, I had an M-80 stuck in the end of a lit cigarette and tossed it on the rear bumper of the paddy wagon. We then pulled nonchalantly through the parking lot and out onto the street. We circled around and parked behind the gas station across the street, and sat there waiting to see what would happen.

It seemed like an eternity. I said to Jeep, "It must be a dud or the cigarette must have gone out, as nothing has happened yet." Just then, the "Suzy Q" donut truck pulled up, and parked just past the rear of Unit 17's wagon. The driver got out of the truck, said hello to the officers, and went to the rear of the truck. Mind you now, he is probably no more than 12 to 15 feet from the rear of Unit 17's paddy wagon. He pulled a lever and down came the power tailgate. He got on it, went into the truck, and came out carrying five large trays of donuts. He pulled the lever and the gate went down to the ground. Just as he stepped off the gate, the M-80 went off. All we could see from across the street was a flash of light and five trays of donuts going skyward. I mean, flying everywhere.

The officers jumped out of the wagon with their guns drawn and were running around the two trucks (being careful, trying not to step on any of donuts).

Once they realized they had been had, they couldn't stop laughing. The poor donut truck driver never did know what happened.

The Russians Have Taken My Daughter

One of the more serious and, at the time, scary incidents I was involved in, while working the West Toledo crew, was a family disturbance call, which is nowadays called Domestic Disturbance. It was a very warm, early spring evening and we were working the 3 to 11 shift.

We were dispatched to a call on Garrison Road. When we arrived, a very upset, petite female in her thirties greeted us in the yard. She informed us that her husband had flipped out and was acting very strange and disoriented. She further stated that he had their seven-year-old daughter and was holding her by the arm and would not let her go. He had told his wife that this was not his daughter and that someone had switched daughters on them.

We entered the house to talk to the subject and, as we walked through the door, he was on the stairs to the right, about halfway upstairs to the second floor. He was holding his daughter with his left hand, and his right hand and arm were pointed at us with something chrome in his hand. He screamed out that we had five minutes to get out of there or he was going to kill his daughter. At first glance, the chrome piece in his hand appeared to be a gun of unknown caliber pointed directly down at us. Jeep and I both ducked behind the wall leading upstairs.

We notified the dispatcher to send a Command Officer and another crew, informing them that we had everything under control but would like a back-up Unit. We asked the dispatcher to inform the crew and Command Officer not to use lights and sirens, as it just might set this guy off. We also asked for an ambulance to stand by, just in case they were needed.

Upon looking around the corner again, we could see that he was holding his wristwatch in his hand. He was screaming that the Russians had entered his daughter's school and switched a girl in place of his daughter and then took his daughter back to Russia. He wanted this girl, who had supposedly been switched with his daughter, to be executed. As we continued to talk with the subject, we slowly inched our way up the stairs and he slowly back-pedaled up the stairs.

When we got to the landing at the top of the stairs, he pulled the girl into the bathroom with him and slammed the door. I hit the door with my shoulder and crashed in, going right through to the other side of the bathroom, right past the subject. As Jeep rushed into the bathroom, the suspect and the girl slipped right past us, turning into the bedroom, just to the right of the bathroom. The suspect attempted to slam the door shut, but Jeep was right behind him and had his foot blocking the closing of the door. The suspect still had the girl by the arm and she was crying and carrying on. Jeep was talking to the subject, trying to reason with him, but to no avail. Jeep, by now, was able to inch his way into the bedroom, just inside the door. I picked up the bathroom door and sat it against the wall and motioned for the wife to ease her way up the stairs.

When the wife got to the landing, I asked her to talk to the daughter and try to calm her down a little. After a few minutes, the wife was able to get the daughter calmed down, but the husband was still carrying on about the Russians switching daughters on him and how this girl must be executed. There was no way we could convince him otherwise.

By now, the other crew and Sergeant were in the downstairs part of the house, as our back-up. Jeep continued to talk to the husband, and the wife continued to calm the daughter. I went downstairs and conferred with the Sergeant and we decided that the only way we were going to be able to end this incident was to take the subject by force. We decided that it would be better if the other crew and Sergeant stayed out of the sight of the husband, until Jeep and I made our move.

I slowly went back up to the landing and informed the wife of our plans. I told her that it looked like the only way we are going to be able to set her daughter free was by force. I told her I was going into the bedroom and that she should watch my actions. When I made a quick move towards her husband, she was to follow and grab the daughter and get her out of there. Jeep and I had worked together long enough that we never had to tell each other what we were going to do. He knew when I nodded my head that we were to attack the suspect.

I slowly entered the bedroom, and Jeep was still trying to talk to the subject, who was still not listening. I could see movement behind me on the stairs so I knew our back-up was in place. Jeep and I were about four feet apart when I saw the father look away at his watch. As he did this, I nodded my head at Jeep, and dove on the bed towards the subject. As I did this, Jeep knew exactly what to do, and he dove at the subject from his location. We both hit the subject at the same time and, in doing so, he released the girl's arm and the three of us collapsed on the bed. Well, you guessed it – the bed gave way with a loud crash. With that sound, the back-up crew entered the bedroom, along with the Sergeant. We had a real scuffle on our hands. Not only had we broken the door to the bathroom, but also the bed and two lamps and a nightstand in the bedroom. It looked like a bomb had been set off in there.

The crew assisted in subduing the subject and getting the cuffs on him. The Sergeant took the wife and daughter downstairs and outside to a neighbor's house to get them away from the commotion.

After getting everything under control, we were able to get in touch with the father's doctor, who arrived at the scene. We took the father to Toledo Hospital, where the doctor signed him into the psychiatric ward.

The wife and daughter were very happy for what we had done for the husband and dad, instead of kicking the shit out of him and taking him to jail. Later that night, we found out that we was a big shot at one of the large companies in Toledo and had just flipped out. Of course, if you hear the other crew's story, they claimed that they had to come and save our ass.

About a year later we ran into the family while we were at another call on Garrison. They all wanted to thank us again, even the father, as he had received treatment and was doing well and was back to work.

Midnight Auto Repair

Officers Ben Klandoff and Harry Sorte were always prepared. If you needed anything, all you had to do was call and meet them. They worked the 8 p.m. to 4 a.m. shift on Unit 584, which was West Toledo. One night about 1:30 a.m., I was working with Jeep again and we were cruising through the church parking lot on Sylvania and Talmadge with our lights off.

We were watching a suspicious car in the gas station across the street. There was one person in the car and one on the outside and I was attempting to see what they were doing.

I wasn't paying attention to my driving and didn't notice that there was a post on either side of the drive and a chain running across between the two posts at the entrance of the drive. I hit the one on the right side of the entrance and I don't know to this day how it happened, but the post ended up in the wheel well and the right front tire was off the ground. There was damage to the right front fender, also. With the noise from the collision, the suspicious car took off. We got out of the car and surveyed the damage.

We knew we were in trouble. I tried backing the car off the pole, but could do nothing but spin the rear tires. We decided to call Unit 584 over and see if they could come up with any solutions. They arrived and, after laughing a few minutes, they told us, "No sweat, we'll take care of you." Harry went into the trunk and got a large gym bag out of the trunk. He pulled an automobile jack out of the bag. We got to work and were able to get the right front of the car far enough up into the air where all we had to do was push the car off the jack, which in turn cleared the pole.

We now had the car off the pole, but what about the damage to the right front fender? Not much, but very noticeable. Next, they brought a large rubber mallet out of the bag and started hitting on the fender. About fifteen minutes later the dent was out of the fender. Now we had the problem of the paint being chipped off. They next took some masking tape out of the bag and put it on the fender. (At this time we had black and white police cars.) Then, out came the black spray paint and they sprayed the bottom of the fender. We waited for about a half hour and then sprayed the top of the fender white.

We still had not solved the entire problem. The number of the car, 418, was on each front fender, right where we just painted. Believe it or not, next came the numerals out of the bag. Thank God they had enough of the right numbers left. The number 418 then went on the right front fender.

Believe me, it was not a perfect job, but no one ever knew the difference.

July 4th ~ Storm Stories

$\mathcal{A}$ very severe storm hit the Toledo area on July 4th one year in the early 70's, while I was working the West Toledo crew. I was working 3 to 11 with Jeep. It seems like I was often working with Jeep when something unusual happened.

We were at the rear of Hiawatha School, finishing up a Malicious Destruction of Property report, when the storm hit. The sky became a very funny, dark brown color and then the wind hit. The trees were bending almost parallel to the ground near us. Then the rain hit. I thought it would never stop.

We drove out to one of the main streets, Secor Road, and were driving north in the 5200 block when we noticed that the headlights were disappearing on all the cars coming at us. Well, that's because they were under water. The water was up to the middle of the car doors. We almost made it through before our vehicle stalled. Just as we stalled, four young males were already out of their cars, and they waded over to our cruiser and pushed us out of the water. All the traffic lights in the whole west end were out.

We were assigned to do traffic at Tremainsville and Alexis (real nice corner to do traffic). By this time, we had taken our gun belts off and placed them, along with our wallets, in the trunk of the car. When we went to work that day, it was almost 82 degrees and sunny, with no mention of any showers, so we were completely unprepared for this type of weather.

There was a police officer who lived in the 5900 block of Rambo Lane. We drove by his house to make sure his wife was okay. Everybody there was safe and sound. The wife gave us four or five large towels so we had something to dry off with every once in a while.

We were dispatched to another district in West Toledo to assist the Rescue Squad and Edison Company. They had an injured man in the water. When we arrived, it was one of the grossest things I have ever seen. There had been a number of kids playing in the water in the street. An electric wire had come loose from one of the poles and was very near to the area where the kids had been. A young male standing by had seen the electric wire and, knowing of the danger, decided to remove it before one of the younger kids got hurt.

When he picked the wire up, it landed on his right shoulder and immediately started burning him. It continued to burn him before anyone could remove it. It cut him right in half, from the right shoulder down the middle of his body to near the crotch area. There was not much blood at all, just one helluva smell. I never saw or have seen anything like that since then. The ambulance removed the body shortly after our arrival.

When we ended our tour at 11:00 p.m., we were informed to take another car out, as we were being held over for another eight-hour shift. This time we were to cover the northernmost west part of the city. The underpass at Detroit and Dura would always flood a lot, even when it barely seemed to rain. We were dispatched to that location to divert traffic away from the underpass. When we arrived at the scene, the water level was the highest I have ever seen it.

Just after our arrival there, a young male was involved in an accident just up the street from the overpass. He was pissed off because the Officers taking the report had issued him a citation. When he left the scene, he took off at a high rate of speed towards the underpass around the barricades and, before he realized that the underpass was flooded, it was too late. His car hit the water and the next thing we saw was him crawling out of the window of his car.

He waded up to the edge, where he was greeted by the original crew that now issued him another citation for

"Driving Around Emergency Barricades". No doubt, this guy was a loser for the night.

When the water finally went down in the early morning hours, we found that there had been three semi's and 11 cars under water. What a mess!!! That was it for the night – sixteen hours and we had to be back to work in another eight hours.

Oh, What A Chase!!

One of the most exciting nights I had while working our crew in West Toledo was on July 29, 1969, on the 11 to 7 shift; and, yes, I was working with Jeep once again. We had just finished a call at an apartment building on Secor just north of Laskey.

We were sitting in the driveway talking to one of the 8:00 p.m. to 4:00 a.m. crews. Along the drive was a row of tall evergreen trees that concealed the apartment building from a car wash next door. It was about 2:30 a.m. and, all of a sudden, we heard the revving of car engines. We could see through the evergreen trees and observed two cars at the traffic light, heading north on Secor from Laskey.

It looked like a real mismatch– a beat-up red-colored early 60's Ford and a newer model, green Chrysler product, like a Barracuda. When the light turned green, the cars took off drag racing north on Secor Road. As they flew past the drive where we were parked, we shot out right behind them with our lights and sirens going. Back in those days, you had to flip a toggle switch and then press on the horn rim and keep pressing it to keep it working, and the red light was a single revolving light on the top of the police vehicle. The 8 to 4 Unit followed right behind us. I was driving and, about a half-mile down the road, the Chrysler product just pulled over to the curb. He knew he had been had and the 8 to 4 Unit pulled over behind him.

The red Ford continued on at a high rate of speed, straight out Secor Road. Jeep and I both stated that we thought he was headed for the Michigan state line, which was only a few blocks up the road. Instead, when we reached the intersection of Alexis Road (two blocks from the state line), he turned right, almost hitting a car as he did, and then took a slight right onto Tremainsville Road.

On Tremainsville, we were reaching speeds of 115 m.p.h. As we were approaching Laskey Road, there was a traffic light and there were three streets that came together at this intersection. The suspect vehicle started slowing down and we thought he was going to stop. Instead, he cut through a service station (almost hitting one of the attendants–full service back then) and back onto Laskey Road, heading west on Laskey towards Secor Road again.

He ran the red light at Laskey at a speed in excess of 85 m.p.h. We slowed down a little as we went through the intersection. We continued on Laskey Road and, near Harvest Lane, I was able to pull alongside him on the left side. Jeep pulled his gun out, pointed it out the window at the driver and yelled, "Pull over, jackoff." With that, the suspect hit the brakes and, as he did so, I continued on a few yards and he made a left turn right behind us right through someone's front yard.

We continued in pursuit down the side streets in a southerly direction. We finally came to the intersection of Monroe Street, which was a main thoroughfare from downtown Toledo into the city of Sylvania. When we reached the intersection of Monroe Street, he turned right and took off again at a high rate, hitting speeds of 95 to 100 m.p.h. He was headed for the City of Sylvania, Ohio, which borders Toledo on one of its westernmost boundaries.

We informed the dispatcher to notify the Sylvania PD that we were headed their way in pursuit of a red Ford. We continued west on Monroe, reaching speeds in excess of 100 m.p.h., as we approached Sylvania. The suspect started slowing down a little in front of the Chevrolet dealership, as the Sylvania PD had the intersection blocked at Monroe and Alexis. He then attempted to make a right turn on a small side street before reaching the intersection that was blocked. As he attempted to do this, his car slid out of control, did a 180-degree turn and the passenger door side of his vehicle crashed into a steel light pole.

We came around the corner just as he slid into the steel pole with a loud bang. He was now facing in our direction as we came around the corner. We looked right at him and he was smiling at us, as he was opening the door to get out. Jeep said to me, "He's going to run from the car!"

I replied, "Bet me," as I slammed his door shut with the front end of our police car, lifting the left side of his vehicle about a foot in the air. Before the car came back down, we were out of our car, along with three or four other officers, pulling his sorry ass from the car and putting cuffs on him. After we had him in a paddy wagon, I stood there and had the dry heaves for about ten minutes. All I could think about were the speeds we were going and crashing the red lights at the intersections we had passed through. I thanked the Good Lord that it was that time of day, and everyone was able to hear our sorry-ass siren.

That was the last real high-speed chase of my career. From that night on, anytime (except once and will get to that later) someone ran on us, once we got the license number, we would stop the chase.

When we went to court regarding this young man, his attorney requested that all charges be handled as an included offense of: No Driver's License. We had written 34 citations against this suspect that night. The Judge said, "Let me look at some of these citations." The first one he picked up was the 115 m.p.h. on Tremainsville, which is a 35-m.p.h. zone.

The Judge then informed the lawyer and suspect that each violation would be tried separately. The suspect received $1500.00 in fines, six months in the workhouse and lost his driver's license for five years. Nothing was suspended. That $1500 was a lot of money for traffic violations back then.

Surprised Burglar

*I*n April of 1975, I was working what was called a make-up day. A make-up day was not a scheduled day off. If you hadn't worked any "make-up days" during the year, you might end up with only six or seven days off when December rolled around. If you were smart, you would make these days up long before the Command started pulling them from you, which would leave you working a day that you really did not want to.

I was assigned to Unit 14, a patrol car in lower South Toledo, working with Paul Price, another classmate of mine from the Police Academy. After fueling the car, we "hit on" with the dispatcher, letting him know that we were ready for an assignment. On day shift, very seldom did you receive a call that amounted to anything at the beginning of your shift.

That morning as we hit on, the dispatcher responded with instructions for us to take a silent burglar alarm at a hardware store on Broadway, just outside the area of near downtown. The dispatcher informed us that we were the only crew available at the time. Normally two crews and a Sergeant were dispatched to that type of call.

I was driving and I turned our overhead flashing lights on, but did not turn the siren on. There was not much traffic at this time of morning and we were able to arrive at the scene in a matter of minutes. I stopped at the front of the store on Broadway and Paul, got out of the car to cover the front of the store and proceeded around the corner and down the alley to the back of the store. There was a garage at the rear of the building that was separate from the hardware store that was used as a storage area. These two buildings were not connected. There were probably 10 to 12 feet between the two buildings and the rear door of the hardware store faced the garage.

I parked in the alley at the rear of the garage and was just getting out of the car to proceed to the rear of the hardware store, when Officer Price came on the radio to inform me that he could see someone in the store moving about. Paul cried out that the person in the store had just spotted him and appeared to be running towards the back of the store with unknown merchandise in his hands. I came around the side of the garage and was approaching the edge of that building facing the rear of the hardware store.

Paul advised me that the suspect was still in the building and appeared to be trying to find a way out of the store. I was able to stand near the corner of the garage and observe the rear of the hardware store. We still had not seen a point of entry to cover if the suspect decided to leave the way he had entered.

I could hear the rear door of the hardware store rattling and I peeked around the corner and could see someone inside the store attempting to get the rear door open but having problems doing so.

I informed Officer Price by radio of what was transpiring. He wanted to know if he should come around to the rear and I told him he had better stay where he was in case the suspect gave up and headed to the front of the store. I told him when the backup unit arrived they could cover the front and then he could come around and cover the rear with me.

Just about that time, the backup Unit arrived and covered the front of the store on Broadway, and Paul started towards the rear of the building. Right then, the rear door of the hardware store opened and the suspect exited the building running with his arms full of items. He was looking behind him at the rear door as he was running. As he reached the area between the rear of the garage, he turned right and then had to turn left around the corner of the garage to head for the alley for his escape.

Right at that moment, Officer Price was coming around the rear corner of the hardware store. I was still standing alongside the garage, Officer Price yelled at the suspect to halt and the suspect turned and looked towards Officer Price as he turned left and headed for the alley. I stuck out my left arm and clotheslined him as he went by, knocking him to the ground. He never knew what hit him. Officer Price and I had the handcuffs on him before he realized what happened.

We placed him in the rear of our patrol car and Officer Price stood by the car while the back-up unit and I checked the building. We were able to find that entry was made on the roof through a vent.

The suspect had numerous electrical tools and the cash register piled up near the rear door. He had two Black and Decker circular saws in his possession when I "corralled" him.

Bit By An Alligator

*I*n the early 1970's, I was assigned to work in the Communications Section for a few months. It was not the coziest place to be in. You worked with seven other officers and it was dark and cold in the office. There were some very good Officers, though, who were assigned to that section. Most of them were older and had had enough of the street duty. We did much of our own cooking, as we had a full kitchen in the office.

I am probably the only Officer in the history of The Toledo Police Department who filed a workmen's compensation report for being bit by an alligator while on duty. Two younger Officers had spent their vacation in Florida and had mailed two small alligators (or whatever they were) to the Communications Office. In these days you were able to mail all kinds of souvenirs through the U.S. Postal Service.

They were both about six inches long when we received them. We kept them in a small aquarium tank that one of the Officers had that his children had used to keep a couple of small turtles in. One of these alligators died about two weeks after we got it. The other one survived and we named it "Alphonse". We would have one of the downtown police crews stop at the bait shop at the corner of Washington and Superior a few times a week and buy us a couple dozen minnows at a time to feed Alphonse.

Our little friend started growing larger and larger. One of the police officers on the street built aquariums as a hobby for a second income. We contacted him and asked him to build one for us. He charged us just for materials, which was in excess of $50.00. All of us assigned to our shift contributed for Alphonse's new home. This was much better for him as he had plenty of room to move around, even though he was still growing very fast. As Alphonse grew larger, we made a leash and collar for him out of paper clips. Each day we would take him out of the aquarium and bring him for a little walk around the office, in order for him to get a little exercise.

Once a week, we would empty and clean the aquarium and give Alphonse a bath. We would take him out of the aquarium and place him in the kitchen sink. We would then clean his "home" and give him his weekly bath. We scrubbed him down with a toothbrush to get all the crud off his body that had accumulated over the week. He had to be held with a thumb and forefinger behind his front legs and his head with one hand at the same time and scrub him with the other.

This was okay until he started growing larger. It was my turn to give Alphonse his bath. He was almost twenty inches long and weighed about three-and-a-half pounds. I lifted him out of the tank and placed him in the kitchen sink. I was holding him by his front legs and head and I noticed what looked like a scab on the end of his nose. I picked him up with my right hand and I started to reach out to touch the scab when ol' Alphonse opened his jaws and decided to grab hold of my left forefinger. I yelped when he clamped down, as it caught me by surprise how fast he was, not to mention it hurt like hell. He broke the skin and I couldn't get him to release his jaws.

I was shaking my hand trying to get him to release, but he wouldn't do it. One of my co-workers in the Office heard me yell and came in the kitchen to see what all the commotion was about. We tried forcing his jaws open, but to no avail. He just kept those jaws closed around my finger. Finally, someone suggested that we try rubbing his belly. Alphonse really liked that, and it was just a matter of a few seconds before he released his grip on my finger. My finger was bleeding, but not very freely. The Sergeant in charge sent me to the hospital where I received a lot of kidding about the incident both at the hospital and within the Police Department. They gave me a tetanus shot because of the bite.

It took a long time for me to live that one down. It wasn't long after that when we donated ol' Alphonse to the Toledo Zoo. He was just getting too big to handle.

The Fishing Expedition
(Or, I Ate the Whole Thing!)

*W*hile working in the dispatcher's office, my co-workers and I had talked several times about going perch fishing on Lake Erie. We decided that we would plan a trip for a time when we all had the day off. We finally found a day that the seven of us were not working. One of the Officers had a connection with the owners of a restaurant/bar on Edgewater Drive in Point Place on the edge of Lake Erie. They owned a boat and the Officer was able to borrow it for the day so that we would have something that would accommodate all seven of us comfortably.

We decided that each one of us would bring something to eat and drink as we would be out on the Lake most of the day. We started out around 6:30 a.m., just as the sun was coming up. It was a beautiful warm day, not a cloud in the sky and very little wind. It was a great idea for everyone to bring food and drink, under the circumstances. However, it became a problem after we got out in the middle of the lake and discovered that we all had brought potato chips and beer. Not very good planning. It was a long day out there on the lake with nothing to eat but salty potato chips. We did catch a number of fish, though, so it was not a complete loss.

After having the fish cleaned, we all went to the Police Post and placed the fish in the freezer there, as they were going to be used for a fish fry sponsored by the Police Post. We were all very hungry after being out on the lake in the sun all day with nothing to eat but the greasy potato chips and beer. At least the beer was cold, as everyone had brought enough ice with them. When we were able to finally sit down at the Post, after putting the fish and equipment away, we discovered that all there was to eat at the Post were Stewart Sandwiches. These are sandwiches that are wrapped in cellophane and placed in a metal-type oven that heats the sandwiches with a lightbulb. Remember, these were the days before microwaves.

We were sitting there eating those God-awful sandwiches and I said to anyone who would listen, "I am so hungry that I could eat the north end of a southbound bull." Mokey Hollenkant, who owned Part Time Cleaners, just around the corner from the Police post, was sitting there half intoxicated, which was his usual state in the mid to late afternoon. He was a very friendly, outgoing and lonesome man.

He heard me make the remark about the bull and he said, "O.J., tell you what, I'll take you to a nice place and, if you can eat the biggest steak they have, I'll buy dinner for everybody here." This was not unusual with Mokey, as many times he would be sitting at the Post, either playing "tonk" or just watching a sporting event, and he would order food for anyone who would eat. He had an account with one of the taxicab companies in Toledo and he would call them and place an order for food at one of the restaurants and then have the taxicab company deliver it to the Post. It was nothing for him to call the world-famous Tony Packo's and order two to three dozen of their Hungarian hotdogs, two to three quarts of chili, and at least a quart of the pickles and peppers. So, when Mokey made the offer that he did, with a little urging (not much, though) from our fishing group, I said, "Mokey, you're on."

He took all of us to Krotzer's Steakhouse on Monroe Street, a place well known for its steaks. It closed in 1997, when it was bought out by a Hooters' franchise. When we arrived, it was apparent that Mokey knew everyone there (he always seemed to know everyone, no matter where you were with him). As we were being seated, he went into the kitchen and, when he came out and sat with us, he told everyone to order except me, as my order had already been placed. When the steak was brought to me, it was the biggest and thickest steak I had ever seen or have seen to this day. The steak hung over the edges of the plate – excuse me, the steak was served to me on a platter. It took me quite awhile to finish it and, thank God, I was as hungry as I was, otherwise I don't think I would have been able to eat it all.

I ate the entire steak, while thinking of the six other guys ready to beat my ass if I didn't finish. Our little fishing expedition did not turn out so bad after all.

Point Place Floods

*I*n the early months of 1973, I finally could take no more of working in the Dispatcher's Officer. The stress in that place was unbelievable. Don't get me wrong – most of the guys were great to work with and we had some good times up there, but I decided that it was time to get back on the street. I was assigned to beat duty in the downtown area for a few months.

Beat duty is probably one of the best jobs on the department and it is too bad that it takes an Officer a few years to realize it. When you are young, you want to go where the action is, in the cars and wagons that answer all those hot calls. Walking a beat district properly, you get to know who owns what business and you become familiar with the people that live and work in the area.

It was April of 1973 and a rainy spring day. I was walking my beat in the downtown area and was told by the dispatcher to stand by at my location, as a Sergeant was going to meet me. The Sergeant arrived in a matter of minutes. He told me I was going to the Point Place area of the City with a few other officers. This area of the city butts right up to Lake Erie. Every time there was a huge storm with a northeasterly wind, the Point Place area would floor unmercifully. This is what had occurred that morning. Officer Richard Zaborowski and I were taken to the Command Post in the Point Place area off of 131st Street. The Chief of Police was there coordinating the evacuation of the homes in the area.

Officer Zaborowski and I were assigned one of the "ducks" operated by the Fire Department. These are large open-type vehicles that have large wheels and can be driven through fairly deep water and also navigated as a boat. On the duck we were assigned to, there were four firemen assigned also. The firemen were all equipped with those wader-type boots that came up almost to their armpits and had straps over their shoulders. The firemen would get out of the duck and rescue people from their home for evacuation. Officer Zaborowski and I stayed on board and would assist people onto the duck.

This lasted just about thirty minutes, as the water was rising fast. The firemen were in the water helping families out of their houses on one side and, on the other side of the duck, there were people screaming for help, as the water was rising around them and in their homes. Officer Zaborowski and I observed a young mother with three small children, two in her arms with water up to her waist calling for help on the other side of the street.

The firemen were all very busy with rescuing people on the opposite side. Officer Zaborowski and I removed our gunbelts, wallets and radios and placed them in a secure place on the duck.

Overboard we went and, as we hit the water the first time, it was a jolt, as the water was very cold. Neither of us had any protective gear or equipment. Our uniform pants were mostly wool at the time and we also wore long heavy coats at this time of the year, so you can imagine how heavy and cold they felt. We were able to get to the mother and children in a matter of seconds and bring them to safety. We stayed in the water from that time on, rescuing more people from their homes. As long as we stayed in the water up to our shoulders, the water did not feel that cold. Walking in the water was a real eye opener for me, though. My legs ached unmercifully for a number of days afterwards, from walking against the fast moving current.

We finally had removed everyone from their homes to safer grounds, but returned to check all the houses again. As we were doing this, we tried to secure each house as best we could. It was useless trying to secure some of the houses, as the water had risen four to five feet deep. We then climbed back aboard the duck and only then realized how damn cold we were. The firemen gave us some blankets to wrap ourselves in, which did not help a whole lot. Our teeth chattered constantly and we could hardly talk, as we were stuttering so bad.

After we were taken back to the Command Post, the Chief took one look at Officer Zaborowski and me and said, "I'm sending you two Officers to the hospital for treatment for exposure. I can't tell where your uniforms stop and your faces begin. They are both the same shade of dark blue."

Upon arrival at St. Vincent's Hospital, we stripped off all of our clothing, and that was a real job, as we were wearing our winter uniforms, consisting of wool pants, long-sleeved shirts and outer coats that were fingertip length and made of a heavy woolen type material. These uniform parts felt like they weighed at least sixty or seventy pounds. What a wet mess they made on the floor of St. Vincent's Emergency Room. We then put on those stylish hospital gowns (of course, mine didn't cover me well) and climbed onto a hospital cart. The nurses covered us with five or six blankets and we were still shaking and shivering like hell.

The doctor on duty came in and examined us. He then said to us with a laughing-type smirk on his face, "I know there is one thing I can give you for this condition, but the problem is that we do not have any here at the hospital. What you two need is a bottle of whisky to warm you up. Since I would be in deep trouble and lose my license if I gave that to you, you're going to have to lay there and warm up slowly."

We were in the emergency room for approximately five hours before they released us. Meanwhile, they had to get in touch with our families to bring some dry clothes to wear home.

That day, Officer Zaborowski and I both learned respect for the power of water. It was a day that we both won't forget.

Taking Care of the Problem

I walked a beat for a few months after working in the Dispatcher's Office and then I was assigned to Unit 4, a paddy wagon in near downtown north Toledo. This district covered most of the near downtown area.

The people on this district only knew one thing, and that was to fight with the police. I was involved in more battles working this district than any other district I ever worked in. We were having a lot of problems with disturbances at the bars in our district. Nothing really serious, but a pain in the ass because, when we did arrive, nine out of ten times, there were no problems.

One of our informants from our district informed us that there was a white male with red hair and he was the one who always instigated these fights. He was known as "Red" but, whenever we arrived, he would always be sitting at the bar drinking, like nothing was going on.

The next few times there were disturbances, sure enough, Red was sitting at the bar, not bothering any-body, but three or four other patrons would be involved in a disturbance. I walked over to Red and told him that the next time we came to a disturbance at a bar and he was in the bar, he was going to jail. A couple of weeks went by and we didn't have any problems.

Later that month, I was working 11 p.m. to 7 a.m. with Office Bryan "Brickey" Chandell, and one of our first calls was for a disturbance in a bar on Ontario Street. When we arrived, the disturbance was still on-going. We then learned from one of our informants that Red had instigated the disturbance, but he had left the establishment when he heard the police had been called.

About an hour later, we were dispatched to the Two Bill Bar on Summit at Locust for a disturbance. We walked in and Red was sitting at the bar drinking his beer like nothing was going on. I promptly placed him under arrest, put him in cuffs and placed him in the back of the wagon. We went back into the bar and tried to quell the disturbance, and almost had it under control, when I turned around, just in time to see a female with her arm raised with a beer bottle going straight at Brickey's head. I grabbed her and placed her under arrest and then all hell broke loose. We really had our hands full, as not only were the patrons fighting amongst themselves, but they were battling with us.

I finally called for assistance, for at least one more crew, as we were not making any headway. Brickey and I were able to get two more patrons in handcuffs before the other crew arrived. When another crew finally arrived to assist, we had already made some progress in clearing up the disturbance, so I notified the dispatcher that we would need at least two more wagons, as we were going to arrest everyone in the place. We arrested everyone, except the bartender, for disturbance and/or disorderly conduct, including one guy who was passed out in the corner on the floor. The total was eighteen arrested.

It took a lot of time to do the all the reports and affidavits, but we never had a problem like that again. Our informant told us that Red had moved out of town, so that problem was solved.

Down Goes The Door

One night, while working Unit 4 in the near downtown north Toledo district, we received a dispatch to meet the Metro Drug Unit Officers at the corner of Lagrange and Champlain. When we arrived there, we were informed that we would be going with them on a drug raid to serve a search warrant on a house in the 1400 block of Ontario.

There were approximately six metro officers and two uniform crews assigned to serve the search warrant. The other uniform crew and three Metro Drug officers were assigned to enter the front door of the residence. Our crew, led by Detective Fred Dodgers, and the remaining Metro Drug officers, were assigned to enter the back door of the residence.

We had a prearranged signal and time to be used when we were to enter the premises. Detective Fred Dodgers was to call out "Police" loud enough so the crews in the front of the residence could hear and then we would count to three before we took down the back door. Remember, this was in the days before they had any type of apparatus to assist you in entering a locked door. The signal went as planned, but when Officer

Dodgers hit the door with his shoulder, it didn't give. Fred called out, "Oh shit, hit it O.J." I was approximately three steps back and I put my shoulder down and hit the door. The whole door came down, doorjamb and all. It sounded like a car or something had hit the house. I went all the way through the kitchen into the counter on the other side of the room, right past the two guys sitting at the table "shooting up", before I could stop my momentum.

They were so high, they just looked up and said, "What the fuck happened to the door, man?" Detective Dodgers grabbed them before they could get rid of the drug paraphernalia. The other crew had hit the front door at the same time and had three in custody in the front of the apartment. They could not believe the size of the hole in the wall where the rear entrance had been. We had one helluva time securing the rear of that entrance before we left the scene.

When you looked at the hole in the back of the house, you would never have guessed that there once had been a door there. Officer Dodgers talked about that incident up until the time he retired.

The Ammonia Spill

On July 10, 1972, I was working the 3 to 11 shift on Unit 4 with Brickey Chandell and it was a hot muggy day. The temperature was in the mid-eighties and the humidity was in the high eighty percent. We were dispatched to assist the fire department with evacuations of homes and were to meet them at the corner of Michigan near Bush. There was a large chemical company near this location that had spilled over five hundred gallons of pure ammonia when it fell off a forklift. We were to go door-to-door to evacuate the nearby residents and tell them to leave their homes until further notice.

We were doing really well with the evacuation, when we observed four or five teenagers running through the field towards the Outward Chemical Corporation, where the accident had occurred. We immediately focused our attention on finding and removing these juveniles from this dangerous area. The grass and weeds in this field were very high and we lost sight of the juveniles. We later discovered that the juvenile suspects had doubled back and got the hell out of there because of the smell.

My partner and I had parked the wagon at the

Command Post and were out on foot searching for the juveniles. As we walked through the field and outlying area, the smell of the ammonia was getting worse and worse. The next thing I knew, my eyes were burning, my armpits were burning, and the crotch area was burning. Any place you perspire is where the ammonia burns. My lungs and throat felt like they were on fire. I couldn't breathe, and I was gasping for breath, as it hurt each time I took a breath. I started back towards the wagon but stumbled and fell twice because my eyes were burning. Brickey was already at the wagon and was also having a difficult time breathing.

I passed out and, the next thing I knew, I was on a stretcher and the rescue squad was pumping oxygen into me. I was taken to the Riverside Hospital Emergency Room for treatment and later transferred to St. Vincent's Hospital, where they had better treatment facilities. My partner's condition was not as serious as mine, so he remained at Riverside Hospital and was admitted. In the hospital, they kept me on oxygen and complete bed rest. My lungs hurt like hell every time I took a breath.

The second day that I was in the hospital, an agent from the insurance company, representing the Chemical Company, entered my room and introduced himself. He wanted me to sign off right there for $500.00. I took a big gulp of fresh oxygen and said I was not feeling very well, and maybe he should contact my attorney. I was in the hospital almost a full week. When I was released from the hospital, I was on light duty for a week and then the doctor released me, as my vacation was starting. To this day, the smell of ammonia really bothers me.

Dukes of Hazzard, Again

I was assigned to Unit 162 in Southwest Toledo, which is a one-man crew. It was a little different at first, working by myself, but at least I did not have anyone to argue with. Never really got into a lot of trouble in these districts, as there was still a lot of farmland around. I did get into a little mess one day, though.

We were having a lot of problems with juveniles operating three-wheel ATV's (all-terrain vehicles) and tearing up the grass at Ryder School on Hill Avenue. Every time we were dispatched to the school, we would arrive and these juveniles would take off at a high rate of speed. As we chased them, they would cross a small creek and go into the cornfield on the other side of the creek. They were able to cross, as there was a small walking-type bridge that they drove over to get away from us. This went on for about three months and, every time we were on days or afternoons, we played cat and mouse with these kids.

One warm summer day, just as I was entering the drive of the school from Hill Avenue, I observed two cycles traveling at a high rate of speed, doing wheelies, and tearing up the grass on the schoolyard. They saw me and took off at a high rate of speed towards the rear of the school where the little bridge that crossed into the field was located. They went across the bridge and sat there taunting me. Unit 161, Officer Paul Wester, had entered the drive right behind me and had observed the actions of the juveniles. He accelerated and drove towards the rear of the school, stopping near the foot bridge.

As soon as I observed the juveniles crossing the bridge, I floored my police car and decided not to stop at the edge of the small creek. I cleared the creek, landing in the cornfield, not more than ten feet from the cycles. The juveniles, stunned by my actions, were still sitting on their cycles when I jumped out of the car to apprehend them. They looked at me in disbelief and said, "You're crazy, man; you're really crazy."

Paul had exited his cruiser as I was doing my "Dukes of Hazzard" feat and joined me in the apprehension. Paul expressed the same sentiments as the juveniles in regards to my actions. The only problem I had was explaining to my Sergeant why I needed a heavy-duty tow for a police car that was not damaged. They had to hook the car up and lift it over the creek. Kind of like what a crane would do. Never had a problem with the three-wheel cycles out there again, though.

Where's the Backup?

I was working Unit 162, a one-man unit in southwest Toledo on the 11 to 7 shift. It was a warm evening and nothing much had been going on. I was dispatched to a disturbance call, along with another one-man Unit in the 4800 block of Airport Highway. It was policy to wait for your back-up Unit to arrive, before you took action on any of the more serious calls. Safety in numbers, they would always say. I arrived on the scene in about three minutes and waited down the street for my back-up, which I assumed would be there momentarily. After a few minutes, I pulled into the drive of the house where the disturbance was reported and a pretty, young female, about 25-years old, came running out of the door of the house in question.

Just as I exited the car, she said to me, "You better get out of here quick. My husband is really pissed off." I said to her, "That's what we're here for, to settle this mess." She said, "But he's really pissed and he's really big." I answered, "Ma'am, I'm not what you really call small, so we'll take care of it."

At that time, I was about 6'1" and pushing 280 pounds. Well, just then, the screen door of the house flew open and off the hinges it went. Through the door came this huge guy, who must have been 6'4" or 6'5" tall, weighing over three hundred pounds. I saw that he had a broken beer bottle in one hand and a large butcher-type knife in his other hand.

I thought to myself, "Oh shit, what did I get myself into now." I asked the dispatcher just how far away my back-up was and requested that he step it up a little. The guy didn't say a word or look my way; he just kept staring at the young lady. When my backup finally arrived, we were able to do some serious talking to the suspect and convince him to drop the knife and bottle. Now that we had that under control, we had him sit down and relax a little and explain the problem to us.

The gist of the disturbance was that they were really having a hard time making ends meet, as he had been laid off from a good construction job, and she was working for minimum wages at some small carryout. She had proposed to him that she become a prostitute to bring in money, just until they got themselves back on their feet. She was really serious about it, and she told us that she had a friend who prostituted temporarily and then acquired a good job.

Later in conversation, we found that her friend was also on drugs and had contacted venereal disease. I can understand why her husband got so upset. Before it was all over, we had them kissing and determined to work it out. There were no arrests made – too much paper work. We never did get any calls from that location again.

The Wedding Party

$\mathcal{D}$uring most of my 34-year career, I worked many second jobs so I could put my two daughters through private schools and then college. The last fifteen years of my career I was in charge of security for the "Greek Festival" in Toledo. This was a three-day event that was very popular in Toledo and was held each year on the weekend following Labor Day. There were times that I had twenty to twenty-five police officers working the festival for crowd control. Sometimes we would get through the weekend without any problems, yet there were some weekends I thought would never end.

One Saturday night, between fifteen and twenty motorcyclists, wearing their colors, came to the festival to do some drinking and have a good time. I told one of the Sergeants, Tyler Stortet, who was working with me, "Damn . . . it looks like we may have our hands full tonight." The motorcyclists were drinking and having a gay old time. Some even went out on the dance floor and attempted to do some of the Greek dances.

A disturbance broke out broke out in one corner of

the festival area, involving five or six people, and a number of the officers responded. As I was working my way through the crowd, I felt a tap on my shoulder and turned around and my head was facing a man's chest. This guy had to have been 6'9" tall, or better, and weighing close to 400 pounds. He was wearing a leather jacket with no sleeves and blue jeans. He said to me, "Officer, if you need any help tonight, just let me and my fellow bikers know and we will assist you." I thanked him and breathed a sigh of relief.

All night long, these guys were always around if there was any problem. At the end of the night, as they were leaving through the gate, we approached them and thanked them and, at the same time, we informed them that we could not let them drive their motorcycles from the festival. I informed them that I had an Officer assigned at the festival all night and that he would watch their bikes. I asked them to walk the cycles up closer to the building, as they were parked about a hundred yards from the property. They grumbled a little bit, but decided that it would be best if they did what we had asked. Their headquarters was only a couple of blocks away, so they all walked home from the festival. They did come back the next morning to pick up their bikes and thanked the Officer who had been there all night.

One Friday night, the festival was really crowded and you could hardly move around in the area. We had been busy all night long and it seemed that everyone was getting drunk from drinking "Ouzo". Ouzo is made from a combination of pressed grapes, and herbs and berries, including aniseed, licorice, mint, wintergreen, fennel, and hazelnut. It is a drink that you are to sip a little at a time.

Well, at the festival, people were chugging this stuff down like water and it was almost an instant drunk. There were numerous small fights all night long, where someone thought he could take on the world after a few shots of Ouzo.

Just around 11:00 p.m., I convinced the chairman of the festival that we should close the entrance gate and not allow anyone else into the festival. He agreed and we closed the gates down for the night. There were a number of persons waiting to get in who protested a little by yelling a few obscenities at us. We usually closed the festival around 11:45 p.m. Right then, a long stretch limousine pulled up near the rear entrance gate and an entire wedding party exited the limo. We were in the process of closing the gates and they wanted to come in. One male in the wedding party, decked out in a tuxedo, attempted to shove his way into the festival. I grabbed him and took him over to the side of the building, getting him away from the rest of the crowd. All the while, his mouth was running that he was going to beat my ass. When I got him over to the side, away from everyone, he became real serious, real fast. All of a sudden, he wanted to cooperate. I asked him for some identification, which he gave me. After checking with Police Records Section by radio to see if he had any wants or warrants, I found that he was known, but not wanted. Since his attitude had changed, I decided to give him a verbal warning and escort him out of the festival grounds. As I was walking him back to the gate, he apologized a number of times for acting so stupid.

As we got closer to the gate, I saw Officers Joe Morton and Tom Rose coming towards me. They had the groom, who was wearing a tuxedo with tails, in hand-cuffs and he was screaming all kinds of obscenities. Joe had him by one arm and Tom the other, as they attempted to remove him from the crowd and commotion near the rear of the main building. The male I had said to me, "I don't want anything to do with this. Can I go now?" I said to him, "Come on, I will walk you to the gate."

As we got to the gate, there were five or six other officers there trying to keep the peace, as this entire wedding party was getting really nasty, while drawing a crowd. Meanwhile, we had notified the police dispatcher that we needed at least one paddy wagon. I continued to escort the male to the outside fenced-in area. As I opened the gate to let him out, the lovely bride lunged at me, grabbed my badge and, in doing so, tore my shirt. The fine young lady in the white wedding dress uttered in her finest voice to me, "I want your fucking badge, buster—you're going to pay for this."

Just then, the paddy wagon pulled up and I notified this young lady that she was under arrest. She swung at me and I took her arm, putting it up behind her back and walked her nicely on her tippy toes to the wagon. The paddy wagon crew then placed handcuffs on her as she continued yelling obscenities at us.

With a little assistance, she was placed in the back of the paddy wagon. As we closed the doors and turned around, five more persons from the wedding party decided to rush us. After a little resistance from them, they were also placed under arrest and escorted into the paddy wagon, where the lovely bride was still uttering obscenities at anyone within view. The paddy wagon officers were just about ready to pull away from the scene, when Officers Mortin and Rose arrived with the groom.

I don't think the bride and groom were entitled to a cell together. They were all charged with assault on a police officer and disorderly conduct.

The limo driver wanted to know what to do, as the wedding party had the limo rented until 2:00 a.m. We informed him he could go down to the Lucas county jail and wait outside for them if he wished, but it would be at least four hours before they would be released. If you were arrested on any charge involving intoxication, you were held in jail for four hours.

Everyone in the wedding party, except the bride and groom, pled guilty when they went to court. We were subpoenaed for a pre-trial hearing for the bride and groom. The case was set for trial after the pre-trial hearing. I subpoenaed six officers and the wagon crew as witnesses. When we went to court, the bride and groom had a change of heart before the trial was to start. They both decided to plead guilty as charged. The Judge decided to read the complete arrest report, which is rather unusual. After reading the report, he stated that they were to spend thirty days in jail on each charge and would be fined $500.00 a piece. He informed them that he would suspend the sentence of jail time under one condition. They were to stand in front of the courtroom and apologize to all the officers involved in this case.

They stood in front of the courtroom and uttered something about being sorry. The judge said that they would have to do it in a louder voice, as he had a hearing problem. They then admitted their guilt and apologized to all of us so that everyone could hear. The judge said that was better and they could leave after paying the fine.

The bride approached me in the hallway later and personally apologized for her behavior that night. I bet they will not forget their wedding night for quite a while. I could have asked them if they wanted their booking photos for their wedding album, but I really am not that cruel.

Lion Store Stories

*I*n 1972, I started working in my off-duty hours as security for the Lion Store, a large department store chain in Toledo. One quick story I remember vividly involved a white male in his 40's, who was observed walking around the store with a shopping bag. You could see that the shopping bag had numerous items in it. I proceeded to watch the subject, as he was acting in a suspicious manner. He went to the book department, picked up a couple of books, placed one back on the rack and placed the other book in his shopping bag.

He proceeded down the escalator and, as he was leaving the store via the mall entrance, I stopped him and identified myself as a police officer and requested to talk to him. I took him into our security room and asked him to remove the book that he had placed in the shopping bag without paying for it. He reached in the shopping bag and handed me a hardcover book. As I took it, I thought I was going to burst out laughing. The title of the book was "I Am Not a Thief," by none other than Richard Nixon.

This suspect had no identification on him, so I had to arrest him and sent him downtown to jail. While searching his shopping bag, we found over $2000 in cash and $3000 in U.S. Government social security checks. Apparently he did not believe in banks. A very strange person.

On another day, I had a juvenile in the security room, whom I stopped for shoplifting. He had no identification on him, so I was trying to check out the name he had given me. He gave me his father's phone number and, as I turned and started to dial the phone, he ran out of the room. He ran to the center of the store towards the mall entrance, with me following as best I could.

I was yelling for someone to grab him. Tom Crasshier, the manager of Men's Suits at the time, was on the floor and observed the juvenile running, with me in pursuit. Tom blocked the entrance to the mall and, when the juvenile saw that his escape route was blocked, he cut back towards the center of the store. At that point, I had a great angle on him. We came together right into a jewelry counter in the middle of the store, breaking the glass display case and sending jewelry flying all over the floor with a loud crash. I pulled him up from the floor and had my forearm around his neck from the rear and was taking him back to the security room. Everyone was yelling at me to put him down. I replied, "I'm not letting go of him until we are back in the security room." I released my grip on him just as we got to the door of the security room and he gasped for air as I let go. Come to find out, when I had my forearm around his neck from the back, I had lifted him entirely off the floor and he was unable to breathe. He didn't run after that. His father was an attorney, but must have decided that his son had it coming, because nothing was ever said and I was never subpoenaed to court.

Another story, I remember well, involved one of the female managers, Sara "Sadie" Worscott. One morning, she was walking through the rear parking lot to the employee's entrance at the rear of the store at South-wyck. Sadie was quite a party-type person and, on this particular morning, she had quite the hangover from the night before. She had parked her car towards the end of the parking lot and was walking through the lot to the employee entrance.

She had walked between some cars to an aisle at the rear of the store and, as she walked between the cars into the aisle way, a car pulled in front of her so that the passenger door was even with her. As she looked up and into the car, the driver, a white male, was sitting in the driver's seat looking at her and masturbating. She said, "You sonofabitch, I don't need this today!" She walked to the front of the car and looked right at his license plate. He backed his vehicle up and took off, with both hands on the steering wheel. Sadie came into the store and informed me as to exactly what had transpired. I took all the information from Sadie and filled out a police report. I then called a police crew, requesting that they pick up the report and turn it in for me.

Right after the store had opened for business that day, Jon Dirtt, Dan Conroy and I went to Frisch's Restaurant, just outside the mall entrance to the Lion store, and had our morning coffee. Sadie was sitting right across from Jon Dirtt and she was explaining to him and Dan exactly what had happened. Sadie reached the part about the license plate and Jon Dirtt had just raised his coffee cup and taken a drink when Sadie said, "Yeah, what I should have done right then and there is turn around and moon the bastard!" Dirtt just about choked before he spit all his coffee out all over the table.

I submitted the report and the Sex Squad called the suspect in for an interview. The story the guy gave was that he had just taken his cat to the vet and the cat had a lot of fleas. He claimed the cat was on his lap in the car and he was getting the fleas off of him when Sadie observed him. Nobody bought the story. His hand was moving awfully fast to be picking at fleas.

He Didn't See The Door

On a very cold night in January of 1977, I was once again working the 11 to 7 shift, Unit 162 in southwest Toledo. This was a one-man unit. I was dispatched, along with another one-man unit, to the Hill Avenue 3000 block for a burglary in progress call.

We both arrived at the scene at the same time – he came from the east and I came from the west. The other Unit pulled around to the back, so I decided I would cover the front. I parked alongside two other cars that were in the front parking area. I turned off my lights and motor and sat there watching the front of the store. In a matter of a few minutes, I could see some movement up near the edge of the building on the west side near the front of the building.

The next thing I saw was a white male with a dark coat and pants running towards the cars in the front parking lot. As he ran, he was looking over his shoulder the entire time, not paying attention to what was in front of him. He was only worried about the police officer in the back of the building. He continued on and started running between the cars in the parking lot right towards me; I could not believe it. Just as he got to the front edge of my car he was still looking back and I nonchalantly opened my car door, knocking the suspect to the ground.

Just at that time, the Sergeant was pulling into the parking lot and observed me picking the suspect up from the ground and putting the cuffs on him. The Officer who was in the back of the building could not believe I had the suspect in custody. Sure beats trying to chase the suspect. So, many times, you just have to be in the right place at the right time and use a little ingenuity to get the job done and outsmart the criminals.

Playing the Right Hunch

On October 8, 1977, I was working a one-man Unit on the midnight shift. It was a nice fall evening, not too cold and not too warm. Another one-man unit and I were dispatched to a house on Westgate Road near Airport and Reynolds Roads for a burglary and possible abduction. The dispatcher said that the suspect vehicle was a dark-colored car with Michigan plates, last seen headed on Westgate towards Reynolds Road. I was southbound on Reynolds from South Street when the description came in. I headed to the scene at a fairly high rate of speed.

When I neared the intersection of Reynolds and Norwich, I observed a black pickup with Michigan plates with a white male driving and a white female as the passenger. I thought, "No, this can't be the suspect vehicle; the dispatcher said it was a car." Then I thought to myself, "I am going to play my hunch and follow the pickup truck."

They turned north onto Reynolds from Norwich and the driver looked at me as he made the turn, a move that told me that this was the vehicle. I made a u-turn on

Reynolds Road, following the subject at a safe distance. He was not making any attempt to run from me, so I just followed him at a safe speed and informed the dispatcher of my location. The dispatcher then informed me that I was following the right vehicle, but to wait for backup as the suspect was supposedly armed and he had taken the female by force.

The pickup truck stopped for the traffic light at the intersection of Reynolds at Hill. When the light changed, I could see my back-up in my rear view mirror, as he had his overhead flashing lights on. As the truck pulled away from the light, I turned my overhead flashers on. When I did this, the driver turned around through the rear window and gave me the finger. I then knew that I was in trouble and I definitely had the right vehicle.

I observed the driver of the vehicle grab the female by the hair and take off at a high rate of speed. As we approached Dorr Street, I tried to pull up on the left side of his vehicle and, as I did, he swerved the truck to the left ramming my car in the right front. He continued on and turned right onto Dorr Street. My backup was now right behind me. As we approached the Inverness Club on Dorr Street, I was going to pull up on his left side again. As I approached, I could see him lean over and it appeared that he was getting something out of the glove compartment. With no way to know what he had grabbed (later found out that it was a large Bowie knife), I backed off a little and kept a safe distance from him. He was probably traveling at about 55 m.p.h. in a 35 m.p.h. zone, so he was not really setting the streets on fire.

As we approached Secor Road, he turned left and, in doing so, he struck two cars that were sitting at the light. When he ran the light at Bancroft and Secor, he hit a few more cars, including a police car trying to block the intersection.

Now there were three or four cars in pursuit of the suspect. As we passed Central Avenue, I informed the dispatcher to notify the North Channel that we were heading north on Secor and would be approaching Monroe Street very shortly. When we reached Monroe Street, there were two police cars there trying to block the pickup. He hit them both and kept on going. As we passed Sylvania, I was at his left rear, another police vehicle was on his right rear, and a third was between us in the middle of his rear.

A fourth Unit, driven by Officer Bob Wast, came around all of us at a high rate of speed and was able to get in front of the pickup and slam on his brakes. The pickup slammed into the rear of the police car and came to a stop as the cars on both sides of him forced their vehicles into his side. Before he knew it, we had him out of the truck and on the ground, as we explained his rights as a U.S. Citizen. I swear we had him out of the truck almost before all the vehicles came to a stop.

His name was Ivan Casterson and he had broken into the house and abducted his ex-wife. I also found out that, when he leaned over on Dorr Street in front of the Inverness, he took out the knife and told her, "If they get me, I'm going to get you," as he waved the knife in her face. He was charged with B & E, abduction and 42 traffic violations. As I recall, he did more time over the moving violations.

Wrong Place To Pull
An Armed Robbery

I remember another incident when the police department received information from one of their informants that the convenience store at Hill Avenue and Wenz Road was going to be held up during our tour of duty.

The officer working the adjoining district, Officer Tim Wanderhilter and I were both pulled from our regular district duties and placed on surveillance inside the store. We were both in full uniform, armed with department-issued shotguns and wearing flak vests. This is before anyone ever heard of the lightweight bullet-proof vests that are worn today. Our vests weighed about 30 pounds each.

We had just finished our tour of duty and the clerk was locking the store up when we heard the broadcast on our police radios concerning a holdup in progress with shots being fired on Byrne & Hill at the ice cream store, which was down the road, about three blocks from where we were. We immediately got in our cars and proceeded to the scene. While on the way, the dispatcher stated that the rescue squad was on the way as they had received a report of one man shot. We were the first crew on the scene. When we arrived, we found a black male lying in the middle of the parking lot bleeding from the chest. There was a revolver in his hand and a cash register money tray next to his body with money strewn all over the ground.

Upon checking with witnesses, we learned that the Bargain City Store at the rear of the parking lot had their own armed security guard. Out front near the street was a small ice cream store called the Ice Stand. The wife of the security guard worked at the Ice Stand. A witness observed the black male pulling the armed robbery and ran into the Bargain City store and informed the security guard of the armed robbery in progress. The guard then ran outside and was standing behind a large garbage dumpster when the suspect come running out of the Ice Stand, cash drawer in one arm and the gun in the other. The security guard then identified himself and yelled for the suspect to halt. The suspect turned and fired, hitting the dumpster. The security guard fired at the suspect and observed the suspect fall to the ground.

Around this time, Sergeant Bill "DaMoe" Moseley arrived at the scene (remember him?) and we could hear the sirens of the rescue squad coming. Bill walked over to the suspect who was gasping for breath, cupped his hands and bent down so only the officers standing there could hear and said quietly to the suspect, "You're dying muthafucker, you're dying." Bill stood up and walked away as the suspect took his last gasp.

The rescue squad arrived shortly thereafter and pronounced him dead. We had to wait for the coroner and it was good ol' Doctor Manderly, who examined the body, declared, "Justifiable Homicide" and then left the scene.

"DaMoe" Moseley just wanted the suspect to realize that justice had been done.

Blizzard of 1978

*I*n January of 1978, the Toledo area was hit with a blizzard that was unbelievable. The night it hit, I was working a one-man crew in South Toledo on the midnight shift. When we went to work that night it was pouring rain, along with lots of wind. It turned to snow around 1:00 a.m. and didn't stop for a few days.

When I got off work the next morning, I had a helluva time getting home. I was able to just get the car onto the drive and into the garage. There were five to six inches of snow on the ground by then. It did not stop snowing and blowing all day. The next night when I had to report to work, I called the desk and told them I needed a ride. By this time, the city was in a state of emergency.

There were a number of volunteers assisting the police and fire crews in the city. Hospital workers, policemen and firemen had to be transported to and from work. A snowmobile had to pick me up at my house and take me to the Southland Shopping Center at Byrne and Glendale, where a police car was available to take me to work. It continued snowing and the wind was blowing at

50 m.p.h. throughout the night. I remember, during the night, turning left from Glendale onto Byrne Road. The wind and snow were so bad, I could not see where I was going. I ended up on top of a snowdrift, unable to get the car off. I called for a city tow truck and was lucky, as he was just down the street assisting another crew. The only problem was this kid was new on the job and, when he hooked the car up to pull me off the snow drift, he only hooked the chain onto the bumper. Needless to say, the car and I were still on the snowdrift and he was driving down Byrne Road with a bumper bouncing in the middle of the street. He finally came back, a little embarrassed, and managed to remove the car from the snowdrift.

I remember another police car had slid off the edge of the road at Hill & Reynolds. Another crew picked up the Officer, as he was informed that it was not known when a tow truck could get out there to assist. He was told to leave his overhead lights on so the car could be seen. I can recall driving by during the night and, before morning, you could not see the car or its flashing overhead lights. It was completely buried in the snow. The crime rate had to be the lowest in the history of Toledo. No one could get out!!

We did nothing but drive around our districts assisting other people. During the night, I was able to stop at the "Big Bear" Food Store in the colony (the only store open 24-hours a day) and get milk and bread for my kids.

When I finished my tour that night, the National Guard had been activated to assist. We had large deuce and a quarter trucks that were assigned just to take officers home and pick them up for work. The nearest they could get to my house was Glendale and Cherry-lawn, which is 7/10 of a mile to my front door. The snow was almost waist deep in the middle of the street by now, and higher elsewhere.

I don't remember how long it took me to get home, but I know I was sore and tired as hell by the time I finally made it there. I had been carrying a grocery bag of the food I had picked up during the night and, when I got to the front door, I leaned on the doorbell. When my wife answered the door, I told her I just wanted to take a warm bath and get to bed.

The next night we were all assigned with a National Guardsman in an Army Jeep. Most of them didn't have heaters, so it was colder than hell riding around in the Jeep. We even had blankets wrapped around our legs. Being as Toledo is the world headquarters for the Jeep Corporation, they gave the City almost 20 brand-new Jeep Cherokees to use during the blizzard.

During the night we stopped by the 7-11 Store on Glendale at Reynolds and there was a heavy equipment operator there who was on a break. He was clearing the snow around Southwyck Mall. He said that part of the mall near the center had collapsed by the weight of the snow. Everything had been closed for three days now, including the Mall.

When I was ready to get off work in the morning, I thought it would be best to get in touch with the superintendent of the Lion Store at Southwyck Mall, where I worked Security during my off-duty hours. I called him at home and told him what we had heard about the roof collapsing at the mall. He said we should get over there and check it out. I called the dispatcher and informed him, and he had one of the Officers, who was assigned a Jeep Cherokee, pick up me and the superintendent and take us to the mall. When we arrived at Southwyck Mall and pulled around to the rear of the Lion Store, it was an awesome sight. You could not see anything at all, except for lots of snow. The snow had blown rooftop high at the rear of the store, yet we could drive up on the sidewalk between the drift and the building. On one side, you had the wall of the store and the other wall was all snow as high as the roof. We were able to get in the store and check it out. Thankfully, everything was still intact.

A few days later, the store was able to open and the parking lot was at least passable, the President (who was not from this area) was standing at the back door with the store superintendent and myself. He said to the Store Superintendent, "I want all this snow hauled away as soon as possible. It does not look good for our customers to see all that snow piled up." I thought the Store Superintendent was going to die laughing. Here the city had been shut down for four days and he wanted all the snow hauled away.

Slowly but surely, the City got back to normal. It was unbelievable how many cars and trucks were buried in the snow – I mean really buried. The grocery stores were still out of a lot of things, like bread, milk, eggs, etc. The trucks still could not get in with the items to make a delivery. I went over to Schoonhill's on Byrne Road to see a friend of mine, Mr. Jerry Gones, who was a butcher there. We bowled together and I usually stopped there in the morning for a coffee. I told him I needed some eggs. They just happened to have some that they were holding in the deli for potato salad. He wrapped them up in the brown meat wrapping paper. That way, no one would bother me, thinking I was getting meat. I had no trouble getting out of the store after making it through the checkout, and no one asked any questions.

Another friend of mine on the department lived on Strathmoor in South Toledo. Since the city was still trying to get the main streets passable, Bubba and all the men who lived in his block of Strathmoor got together and made a large bonfire in the middle of the street. They then went to work shoveling the streets of the snow. The wives brought out tables and chairs, food and, of course, refreshments for the men. It was one big party!!!

They were the only ones that had their entire street cleaned. It just shows that things can get done when you put your minds together and work together and have fun doing it. The morale on the department was almost as high as it was during the civil disturbances of 1967.

Just Checking Out A Room

*W*hile still working the one-man car in the Southwyck area, I was patrolling one night and was dispatched to the Toledo Motel on Reynolds Road for a "peeping tom". I was close to the location, so I arrived in just a few minutes. I pulled in with my lights off and went into the office. This was a small hotel, just one floor with 45 to 50 rooms. The night clerk said that the peeping Tom was still there and was out back between two buildings. The rear of the rooms backed up to each other, with about twenty feet between them.

The night clerk told me to go out the door and go to the rear of the office and then turn right. This was about 75 feet from where I was. I started back that way and, when I got to the corner of the building behind the office, I looked around the corner and I could see someone between the buildings.

I stepped back a little, put my keys that were on my gun belt in my back pocket and then unsnapped my gun. I looked around the corner again and could see a male leaning up against the building with his left hand. His left rear side was facing me, so he could not see me. I edged along the back wall of the other side of the motel, until I was approximately twenty feet away from him. Now I could see what he was doing. He had his left hand on the wall looking into the room and was masturbating with his right hand.

I took my gun out of the holster and brought it up to eye level. I pulled back the trigger and, as it clicked, I said, "I don't think I would move either of your hands at the present moment. This is the Police and you are under arrest." He stopped in mid-stroke and did not move either hand. I came up behind him and told him that now he could put his right hand on the wall also. I then cuffed him and started back to the car with him. He asked me, "Can I stop and put it back in my pants?" I told him, "You're so proud of that, why don't we just let it hang out till we get downtown, because I sure as hell am not going to help you tuck it in."

When we got to court a few weeks later, I found that he was an air traffic controller at the airport. Just the type of guy I would want guiding my plane in for a landing!

Playing A Hunch, Again

*I*n December of 1978, I was working a one-man unit around the Old Orchard area, near the University of Toledo. We had been having numerous residential burglaries in the area. It seemed that, every day, I was taking at least one or two reports, and they were all happening between 9:00 a.m. and noon.

All of the burglaries were corner houses and entry was made by breaking a small window at the rear of the houses to allow them to either open a window or door. I was able to have fingerprints lifted from a few of the places. I started putting all these things together and went to my Captain. I asked permission for an unmarked vehicle to use in that area for a few weeks to see if I could come up with something. He told me he would give me two weeks.

Staying within the boundaries of Kenwood to Bancroft and Secor to Cheltenham, I started keeping track of the different cars I could see driving through the area. I then would run registrations and see if the owners had any records, because I was looking for one that fingerprints could be compared to.

I observed one car within the area three or four times in the first three days. The next time I saw the car, there were two black males and a black female in the car. I asked for a marked Unit to watch for the car. The marked Unit saw it run a stop sign at Meadowood and Christy. They stopped the car and got names and other pertinent information on all the occupants. One passenger was wanted on warrants and had no record. The other two were known, but not wanted.

I got in touch with Detective Bob Tomason and told him that I suspected three people and I thought he should check the fingerprints against the fingerprints we were able to get from some of the houses that had been burglarized. About two days later, Bob called me and said we had a match. After it was all over, Bob ended up with 57 clearances of burglaries in the West Toledo area. Needless to say, I felt real good about that one.

What A Surprise!

When I was first assigned to the Records Section, we had a Sergeant who was a little different. Very likeable, but different. One problem with Marvin was that he wanted everyone to know that he was actually the one running the Records Section, not the Captain.

Marv like to flaunt his money all the time, also. He always had to have the best of everything. When VCR's first came out, Marv had to have two of them. Marv also liked to make a move on all the good-looking girls, whether officers or civilians.

In the Tab room, there was a black female named Phyllis Jarkason who was a real trip. Her outfits were outrageous. She would wear jump suits that were one-half purple, the other half white. She would then wear one white shoe and one purple shoe. On one hand, her fingernails would be painted in white, with the other in purple. Her earrings would be one purple and one white. All of her outfits were like this. She had more chin hairs than most men I know.

On Secretary's Day one year, Sergeant Marvin Sabbath sent all of the females in the Records Section and the Tabulating Room office a red rose in a vase. All of the cards were blank inside and the names of the girls were on the outside of the little envelope, except the one that Officer Lorie Marsont was to receive. We were working the 3 to 11 shift when these flowers were delivered for the next day.

We could see that Lorie's had writing on the card inside the envelope (by looking real close through the envelope) and that the others were blank. The Sergeant working the afternoon shift decided to slit open the bottom of Lorie's envelope to see what it read. The card inside read, "Roses are red, Violets are blue, I can't wait to have dinner with you."

We thought that was very touching, but thought maybe it should be addressed to someone else. We were able to find another envelope and put the card with the note in it and put it on Phyllis's Desk. The afternoon Sergeant, along with one or two other Officers, inserted the blank card on the vase on Lorie's desk.

The next day Phyllis kept winking at Marv, giving him looks that you would not believe. Lorie never mentioned anything to Marv and, about halfway through the shift, Marv could not take the suspense any longer and called Lorie into his Office and asked her how she liked the rose in the vase. She said it was very nice of him to give the roses to all the girls. Marv then asked her if she liked the note on her card in the envelope. She told him that she had no idea what he meant and explained that her card was blank. Marv knew right then that he had been had by the best. Phyllis approached him later and asked him if he was serious about taking her to dinner. Marv really had to do some talking to get out of that one.

Marv could never figure out who got him on that one, because other Sergeants and Officers on each of the shifts liked to pull things on him.

Christmas Charity at The Lion Store

*I*n the late to mid-1980's, Lion Store Southwyck, where I worked part-time as an Off Duty Police Officer, started a charity function at Christmas time. Every year, the Lion Store would sponsor between twelve and fifteen needy families in the area. The Department Managers would organize the function, with help from employees in their respective departments. Money was raised by raffling off numerous items to the employees at the store and then awarding them at a breakfast for all employees.

The President, along with the Superintendent of the store and all the Department Managers, would get up on a Sunday morning and go to a rental hall at 4:30 a.m. to cook the breakfast for this fundraiser. The following week, Department Managers would get the lists of the families from an organization in the City that handled these matters. They then would proceed to buy food and presents for the entire family. There would be enough food purchased to last three to four weeks, if used correctly. Each person in the family would be outfitted from head to toe with a new set of clothes, along with two or three toys for each child in the family. After the shopping was completed, everything was gift-wrapped (except the food items) and organized for each family. A day was then scheduled to deliver these items to the families in question. The families would be notified as to what day we would be arriving.

We usually had two semi-trailers with the presents and food and three to four carloads of volunteers to help deliver the gifts. Since I had been the unofficial store "Santa" for most of the store parties and Breakfast with Santa over the last few years, I was asked each year to also be involved in this activity. This was done as a volunteer in my off-duty hours.

Upon arrival at each house, Santa and one or two of the Managers (wearing hats like Santa's Elves) would go to the door and announce our arrival. After Santa entered and wished each and everyone there a Merry Christmas, the rest of the volunteers (Elves) would begin bringing in the items. Santa would then give each child one gift that he or she could open that day, and instruct them that the rest of the gifts should not be opened until Christmas morning. Most of the people whom we helped really appreciated what was being done for them. There were others, though, who acted as if it was expected, and others who felt that they should have more. We went to one home in North Toledo that really had us all upset. As we were leaving, we were asked, "Is this all you are going to give us? We thought there would be a lot more."

The one house that we went to that stuck in everyone's mind was one in lower North Toledo. We had two brand new buyers that worked at Lion Store for only a short while and they volunteered to go along with us. These two new female buyers were fresh out of college and I do not think they were ever exposed to anything that we, as police officers, had encountered. They were about to get a lesson on what the real world can look like. We had already delivered to seven or eight places on this day, when we headed to an apartment building at the corner of Superior and Locust.

When the door opened, I knew from past experiences as a police officer, that the place was going to be different than most we had entered that day. This place was a filth hole!! The sheets on the bed were so dirty that we could not tell what color they were. Every step that we took in the house, we could hear the cockroaches crunching under our feet. Plates were in the sink and we could see creatures crawling on them. I swear the fleas were jumping three feet into the air. Well, Santa did his job passing out gifts, but when I turned around, the only people left from our group were two of the male furniture salesmen and myself.

Like I said earlier, there are usually 12 to 15 people on this Mission of Mercy. They all carry the gifts in and then usually stand around and watch the proceedings as Santa does his thing. And, as always, we take pictures of Santa passing out the goodies.

Well, this time, just about everyone had abandoned Santa. After we wished the family a Merry Christmas and went outside, our two buyers were still brushing themselves off, along with having the dry heaves and saying that they could not believe the condition of the residence. The fleas were still jumping a foot high when we got outside. I have to admit it was one of the worst I had ever seen. It was something that was talked about for many years to come.

Geek of the Week

*I*n the 1980's, the Chief's Office of the Police department would name both an Officer and Command Officer of the month. The Officer's name and assignment, along with his picture, would be placed on a bulletin board on the first floor of the Safety Building for everyone to see.

A month or so after this started, some unknown person started posting the photocopy of an officer (could be a patrolman or command) and this person was named "Geek of the Week". This person did not have to do anything special, it was just someone picked out by an unnamed person within the employment of the Safety Building. No it was not me, as I was nominated one month, but I do think I know who it was, as I caught one person putting up a "Geek of the Week" notice early one morning.

This went on for quite some time and brought smiles to employees working in the Safety Building. People from the Chief on down to patrolmen were named as "Geek of the Week". The Chief at the time, Marvin

Fleckner assigned his assistant, Lieutenant Raymundo Natendio to check on the first floor two or three times each day to take down any "Geek" paraphernalia. Raymundo would sneak down the old prisoner elevator, hoping to catch someone doing it. There were times he would check and not find anything, but within minutes the "Geek" paraphernalia would be back in place. This little mystery just about drove him nuts.

I do not think he ever caught who was doing it, but after a while it stopped. Are there any older police officers or anyone working in the Safety Building at the time that know who was doing the dastardly deed? If you know, send me a note, as I am curious as to who might have been spending their time frustrating Lieutenant Natendio.

An Embarrassed Classmate

I was assigned to the Police Records Section the last years of my career. I was handling all the towed vehicles within the City. One Monday during the day shift, we were busier than hell at the Records Section. Everyone who had their vehicle towed, and persons wanting to make police reports, showed up to take care of business at the Records Section. Crews were not usually sent to minor calls, unless the victims insisted on seeing a crew at the scene.

On this particular day, it was extremely busy, the phones were ringing off the hook and there must have been at least seventy-five to a hundred people in the hallway waiting to make a report or get their vehicle released from being impounded. I had stepped out into the hallway to go to the Auto Squad office to check information on a vehicle that had been towed in for an investigation.

As I was walking through the area I heard someone call out "O.J., how the hell are you?" I looked up and it was an old grade school and high school classmate of mine, Mike Burkett. Mike had always been a prankster in school and I thought to myself, I am about to get even with him for some of the things he pulled during our school years.

I said to him, "Hi Mike, how have you been?" He replied to me "Great, but I need some help. While I was away over the weekend, they towed my car– can you help me out? I said to him, as I continued on walking towards the elevator, "I'd like to help you out Mike, but I am on another assignment right now."

Then I replied to him, rather loudly, so it could be heard by everyone, "By the way, Mike, how did you come out on those child molestation charges you had pending, were you able to beat them, AGAIN?" The expression on his face and the faces of other people in the area was priceless. You could see everyone backing away from Mike, while mothers put their arms around their children and turned away from Mike. I continued on to conduct my business at the Auto Squad.

Where's the Money?

$\mathcal{D}$uring my last ten to twelve years on the Police Department, I became active in the Police Credit Union and was elected to the Board of Directors. When I first joined the Credit Union, the Office was in the Safety Building garage and had just one room for one worker and one customer at a time.

Over the years, the Credit Union grew very fast with the addition of Officers and families to the membership and with additional services offered. Finally, one year, the Credit Union was able to move from the hole in the garage to the first floor of the Safety Building. At the time there were three employees and a Manager. The Credit Union growth continued and it wasn't long before the Board of Directors decided that an additional office was needed to better serve the membership. After many months of study for a location and building, we were able to buy a building that once housed a bank branch in South Toledo.

An enormous amount of work had to be done on the building, as the interior was decorated from the 70's and was dark and gloomy. New teller stations had to be constructed along with new paint, wallpaper, carpeting and a new manager's office. The manager at the time was Larraine Walczak Kern, now known as Larraine Walczak Kern Ford, who was very much involved in the remodeling of the entire place. Many nights and weekends, she was there working until the wee hours of the morning, overseeing the construction and remodeling of the building. I was appointed by the Board of Directors and put in charge of the entire remodeling and, along with Ms. Walczak, put in many hours completing the project.

In late March of 1995, we were winding down with the remodeling of the building and were approaching the Grand Opening date that we had set for April 2nd. On the Friday before the grand opening, we had everything scheduled to be delivered to the new branch office. Appliances for the kitchen and break area for employees and the new safe, along with furniture, were to arrive. We were able to purchase a safe from the Lion Store for $50.00, as they were disposing of it, as they had to purchased a bigger one. We also had the locksmith scheduled on this day to change the combination on the safe for us.

Money had to be transported to the new branch office so that it would be ready on Monday morning when we opened for business. Larraine and I decided that we would pull my car into the Safety Building garage and we would put $286,000.00 in sealed money bags into the trunk of my car. We would then have Larraine drive her car, and I would follow her, with a Police Sergeant following both of us to the new building in a marked car. We never let on to anyone how much money we were taking to the new office. Everything went as planned and we arrived at the new office at around 2:00 p.m.

When we arrived, there was all kinds of activity going on. The furniture and appliance people were there with the new furniture and the safe was on the back of a tow truck in the front yard. One of the members was a retired Officer and had volunteered to deliver the safe for us. Larraine and I immediately got out of our cars and went to work directing the people on where to put the each item.

We had a real problem getting the safe into the building. We had to remove a couple of boards around the door jamb to be able to just squeeze the safe through the door. Once inside, we then had to maneuver the safe into place. Before we knew it, it was almost 6:00 p.m. The only ones still around were Larraine and myself. It had been a very unusually warm day and I was beat. As the day wound down, I remembered that I had to be in

Ypsilanti at Eastern Michigan University by 8:00 p.m. I mentioned this to Larraine, as we were sitting in her office having a can of liquid refreshment. She told me to go ahead and she would wrap up a few things in her office and head home for the night. She said we could finish anything else on Sunday afternoon, as everything looked to be in place.

In this period of time, cellular phones were nowhere near as popular as they are today. The Credit Union had purchased a bag phone that we were using during the remodeling phase and I had it with me the last week or so of the remodeling, so that anyone involved with the remodeling could get in touch with me. Larraine did not want it with her as she had enough to worry about with the day-to-day operations of the credit Union.

I left the new credit Union office and headed home to change clothes and head for Ypsilanti. On the way home, it hit me like a ton of bricks that I still had all the money in the trunk of my car. I started to panic as I did not know what the hell to do. All I could envision was me getting in a rear-end collision on the way to Ypsilanti and having money strewn all over the highway or getting stopped by the Michigan State Police and having my car searched. I'm sure it would have been harder than hell to explain cash in the amount of $286,000 in the trunk of my vehicle. As I was thinking of this, I broke into a cold sweat. I remembered that I still had the bag phone, so I plugged it in and called Larraine at the Office. Thank God, she was still there. I told her what we had forgotten and offered to drive right back. I arrived back at the new office and backed my car right up to the door and we removed the money and placed it in the safe and locked it up immediately. I then breathed a sigh of relief.

Larraine and I still have a good laugh about this incident till this day, but it sure was scary as hell that night. That bag phone was a very useful tool that night.

Santa Learns the
Meaning of Christmas

The most memorable Christmas deliveries that I made while employed at the Lion Store made me and the other volunteers think about the real meaning of Christmas.

Years later, when my daughters were in high school, I told them about one of the visits. It really stuck with them and, to this day, they remember the story vividly. My oldest daughter, Julie wrote about it in her high school newspaper in her junior year and received many comments from school officials and students on the story.

On this delivery for our Christmas Charity function, one of our stops was at a small yellow twinplex on Tremainsville Road in West Toledo, right across from Start High School. This was a mid-class neighborhood and the twinplex was in fairly good condition. We knocked and announced that we were from Lion Store and had some Christmas gifts for the family.

The mother answered the door and she appeared to be in her mid-twenties, thin, with shoulder-length blond hair and moderately dressed. There were three children, a boy about six or seven, a girl about three or four and another boy about two. As we entered, you could see that there was not much furniture, but the place was very clean. Like they say, you may be poor, but you can be clean. In one corner there was a small black and white television sitting on a very old table. There was one worn couch and chair in the living room, along with two metal folding chairs.

In the front window there was a three-foot tall Christmas tree on a wooden crate. This tree looked like the Christmas tree from the comic strip Charlie Brown. Most of the branches were bare and there were just a few ornaments on the tree and no lights. The ornaments were tin can lids that the children had apparently decorated. On the tree was one small candy cane.

The mother immediately started crying and the tears really flowed down her cheeks when she saw all the food that was being carried into the house. I mean a whole turkey, ham and everything else to go with it, plus a lot of the basic foodstuff needed on a daily basis.

She hugged Santa and said, "Thank you for giving us a perfect Christmas." Santa then proceeded to give each of the children a gift to open and made them promise that they would not open the others until Christmas morning. All three of them squealed with glee when they opened their one gift and they all jumped up and hugged Santa, saying, "Thank you Santa." The mother was still sobbing uncontrollably, saying over and over what a perfect Christmas it was going to be.

As I was walking out of the door waving and saying Merry Christmas to everyone, the oldest child went over to the Christmas tree and took that lone candy cane from the tree and then cried out to Santa, "Wait a minute Santa, we've got something for you." He then ran across the room to where I was standing in the doorway and held the candy cane up to Santa and said, "This is for you Santa. Thank you for making our Christmas a good one."

Let me tell you, that really choked up this big guy; I had tears in my eyes, along with everyone else, all the way to the next stop. To this day, every time I drive by that little twinplex, the thoughts of that day cross through my mind and I think of what the real meaning of Christmas should be to everyone.